ND THE WORLD YACH

PACIFIC OCEAN

INDIAN OCEAN

AUSTRALIA
Fremantle

NEW ZEALAND
Auckland

D ISLAND

SOUTHERN OCEAN

Courtesy of ANZ

▶ Leg 4
5914 Nautical Miles
AUCKLAND to
PUNTA DEL ESTE (URUGUAY)

▶ Leg 5
5475 Nautical Miles
PUNTA DEL ESTE to
FORT LAUDERDALE (USA)

▶ Leg 6
3818 Nautical Miles
FORT LAUDERDALE to
SOUTHAMPTON (ENGLAND)

GLEN SOWRY

Growing up on the shores of Paremata Harbour instilled in Glen Sowry a passion for yacht racing. From humble beginnings in the ubiquitous P class, Sowry won national titles in various classes before moving into the tough Olympic 470 class, where he competed with distinction in numerous international events.

The 1985/86 Whitbread race provided Sowry with the opportunity to sail on *Lion New Zealand*. He established himself as a top-class helmsman and sail trimmer. Sowry rejoined Peter Blake on board the all-conquering *Steinlager 2*, before heading to San Diego to join the New Zealand America's Cup team.

Throughout the last nine years he has written regularly for several publications worldwide. He co-authored with Mike Quilter the best-selling book *Big Red*, the story of *Steinlager 2*.

Glen and his wife Sandy live in Auckland.

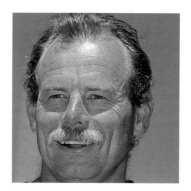

GRANT DALTON

Grant Dalton's name is synonymous with the Whitbread race. His first taste came in the 1981/82 Whitbread when he joined *Flyer* on her winning circumnavigation. With this background, Peter Blake recruited him to sail on *Lion New Zealand* as a watch captain.

The 1987 America's Cup beckoned and he formulated plans for his own Whitbread campaign — what was to become *Fisher and Paykel*. Dalton forced everyone to sit up and take notice with his impressive second placing in his first race as a skipper. The experience and knowledge gained from his first campaign as skipper were to form the basis of the *New Zealand Endeavour* campaign.

Dalton co-authored with Pat Hanning *Come Hell and High Water*, the story of the *Fisher and Paykel* campaign.

Grant lives with his wife Nicki and daughter Eloise in Auckland.

ENDEAVOUR

WINNING THE WHITBREAD

GLEN SOWRY
GRANT DALTON

Hodder & Stoughton
A member of the Hodder Headline Group

Cover and text design by Dexter Fry
Typesetting by Egan-Reid Ltd
Edited by Richard King
Proofread by Hilly Wilson
Printed in Singapore by Kyodo Printing Co. for Hodder & Stoughton, a division of Hodder Headline PLC, 44–46 View Road, Glenfield, Auckland, New Zealand.

Contents

Acknowledgements

There are numerous people I wish to thank for their contribution in helping to bring this book to fruition.

Peter Rotgans provided a valuable insight into the tentative early days of the campaign. David Glenn of *Yachting World* (UK) and Andrew Mitchell and Geoff Green of *Boating World* allowed me to adapt material I had written for their magazines. John Lusk of Russell, McVeagh, McKenzie, Bartleet and Co. provided valuable legal advice. Christine Moffat from Hodder Headline helped to keep the project on schedule, while Rick Tomlinson from *Intrum Justitia* and Hans Bernard of *Merit Cup* generously supplied us with photographs.

Most importantly, a special thank you is due to my wife Sandy for her constant enthusiasm and constructive criticism over the months it took for this book to evolve.

Glen Sowry

We are grateful to the photographers whose work is represented in this book, and acknowledge the assistance of the following photographic sources:

Allsport: pages 47, 48, 65, 86, 106, 123, 162–163

Kevin Batten: pages 54, 65

G. Green, Boatworld: page 34

Carlo Borlenghi: pages 53, 60–61, 63

David Branigan: pages 1, 51, 110, 134, 160

Fotopacific: front cover

R. Guerrini: page 92

Mike Hewitt: pages 1, 108, 140, 159, 175

KOS: pages 111,118

Merit Cup: pages 104, 117

Steve Munday: pages 170–171, 173

New Zealand Endeavour: pages 2, 8, 12, 16, 17, 18, 19, 20, 23, 25, 27, 29, 30, 31, 32, 33, 36–46 (incl.), 58, 59, 66, 69, 71, 73, 75, 76, 78, 79, 80, 81, 82–83, 84, 87, 89, 91, 93, 94–95, 98, 100, 105, 113, 115, 124, 127, 133, 136, 138, 141, 142, 143, 145, 146, 147, 149, 152–153, 154, 156, 164, 166, 167, 168, 169

Photosport: page 23

Gary Prior: pages 121, 122

Rick Tomlinson: pages 102–103

Jeppe Wikstrom: page 56

Yamaha: pages 150, 156

The Skipper's Log

'Watch me next time' were the final words of *Come Hell and High Water*, the book about the *Fisher and Paykel* campaign. *New Zealand Endeavour* was an idea that was started almost immediately after the completion of the previous Whitbread. This time it was going to be tough to get the money, but my wife Nicki's support through what was to become the hardest period of my life made it possible to keep going.

Before we could go out looking for money, we had to get the concept right. Three people stand out from this difficult period: Julian Mounter, the former CEO of TVNZ, Peter Rotgans, formerly of McCann Erickson, and Ross Armstrong.

Throughout those early months, Peter and I spent many hours working on the concept. Julian provided the critical TVNZ component, and Ross used his extra-ordinary network of political and business contacts to open doors. It is in some ways unfair to so many other fantastic people to single these three out. However, without their input we would never have got started. I owe them a debt of gratitude.

Throughout the course of the campaign many others played a significant role in our ultimate success, donating their time, expertise and enthusiasm. They included John Lusk, Tony Ebert, Gary Paykel and Don Rowlands. Some may not find their names in this book, but all should take pride in the fact that it was due to their collective input that we were successful.

In the end it was the 'Magnificent Seven' corporates, along with TVNZ as the official broadcaster, that brought *New Zealand Endeavour* to life. They had the vision and courage to commit to the project and, without exception, were great to deal with. They were never overbearing and showed incredible levels of enthusiasm for the campaign.

For me, as skipper, the campaign was everything I had hoped it would be. At the core of it was a team that functioned as a coherent unit and was dedicated to the winning of the race. I am often asked to speak on motivation — how do you keep them going? What are the secrets? Frankly I have no idea — it all just seems to happen. Select the right people, make sure everyone knows what's expected of them, define the goals (long and short term) and, despite minor hiccups along the way, the rest will just happen. If I've learnt any lesson over the years, it would be to let people get on with their jobs but sort out problems, quickly and decisively.

It is not commonly known that *New Zealand Endeavour* was the only yacht in the Whitbread fleet that didn't change its crew during the race and that it was the only true national entry in the race. The strength of that team ruled supreme.

This book is ultimately dedicated to the thousands of New Zealanders who joined our Supporters Club, watched the arrival on television through the night, came down to welcome us into the Viaduct Basin, stopped me in the street to say 'Well done', wrote me letters or were glued to the nightly Whitbread Report.

Grant Dalton

CHAPTER ONE

The Long and Winding Road

On 22 May 1990, a huge New Zealand flag flew proudly in the warm English afternoon sun, as beneath it an impressive big red boat and her fifteen-man Kiwi crew, led by Peter Blake, slid across the Southampton finish line to complete their dominance of the Whitbread race. On board *Steinlager 2*, the crew's relief and exhilaration of finally having achieved their goal was immense. For Peter Blake, the moment was particularly satisfying; it was the culmination of twenty years of chasing his dream of winning the Whitbread.

Only half an hour later, another Kiwi ketch ghosted across the finish line in the dying afternoon breeze, to claim a decisive placing of second overall for the race. At the helm a young New Zealander and his crew lowered *Fisher and Paykel*'s sails for the last time as they prepared to join *Steinlager 2* in the crowded harbour. For Grant Dalton, the short journey from the finish line to the arrival pontoon was one of very mixed emotions. While his performance at having finished a creditable second in his first attempt as a skipper was sufficient reason to hold his head high, there was the gnawing ache of knowing that he had not achieved the goal he had set himself some years earlier.

As *Fisher and Paykel* pulled alongside its arch-rival in Southampton's Ocean Village, the deep-seated respect between the two Kiwi crews was evident as we shook hands. Even then, we knew if New Zealand was to win the Whitbread race again in four years' time, it would be a combination of these two crews that would form the nucleus of that team.

Grant Dalton had made a decision to mount another challenge for the Whitbread by the time he stepped ashore in Ocean Village. That was to prove to be the easiest part of the project. Coming up with the $14 million that would be required to compete in the next race was an infinitely tougher proposition altogether. New Zealand was in the midst of a tough economic recession and many of the larger companies and corporations were being forced to restructure. Despite the dominance of *Steinlager 2* and *Fisher and Paykel*, and the massive awareness and commercial value these two sponsors achieved, the prospect of finding the capital required to fund a new Whitbread maxi in this financial climate, was akin to finding the proverbial needle in a haystack.

While immersed in the task of selling and handing over *Fisher and Paykel* to her new Italian owners, Grant began to assemble the team of marketing and business brains he would need to help him put a new campaign together. Until he was confident that he would achieve the necessary financial backing, there was little point in getting too immersed in the intricacies of boat design. That would be relatively easy work, which could proceed quickly once the financial muscle was at work.

New Zealand Endeavour *sheds her skin as the mould is lifted out of the hull shell.*

Those people Grant gathered around himself to assist with the complex task of securing sponsorship were to invest hundreds of hours of their time in the following months pursuing their goal. Grant and his fellow 'think tank' members, Peter Rotgans and Ross Armstrong, set about devising a strategy that would attract potential sponsors. With the additional guidance of Fisher and Paykel Chief Executive Gary Paykel and Don Rowlands, this small team spent countless hours thrashing ideas around on a whiteboard as to what shape and form the whole sponsorship package should take.

For Grant, the intricacies and dangers of racing a maxi ketch through the rugged Southern Ocean paled into insignificance alongside the daunting task of undergoing a crash course in the marketing business. Peter Rotgans, who was at the time working for the advertising agency McCann Erickson, spent many long after-work hours and every weekend working alongside Grant, putting together the plans and organisation that would ultimately get us to the start line.

Peter's wife Gale must have often wished she had never heard the word Whitbread, as the weekends of solid work went on month after month. Ross Armstrong was a great help throughout these tentative stages, with his political contacts and strategic thinking. Grant spent many hours in counsel with Ross, discussing the finer points of the emerging package.

However, in this embryonic stage of the campaign, it was Peter who was to pull all of the loose strings together, finalising the all-important formula and writing sponsorship proposals. His first taste of the Round the World yachting business came back in 1984, when he assisted Peter Blake's *Lion New Zealand* campaign, followed four years later with an even deeper involvement in the *Fisher and Paykel* project. With all of this experience behind him, Peter probably knew more about Whitbread boat marketing than anyone else in New Zealand.

The final key player in the fight for sponsorship emerged in the form of Julian Mounter, then Chief Executive of Television New Zealand. Having witnessed the spectacular dominance of the Kiwis in the last Whitbread race, he was concerned with the tendency of New Zealanders to take their top sports performers too much for granted. Although he is a Pom, Julian was adamant that New Zealand should be represented again in the next Whitbread race.

Julian and Television New Zealand were to become the catalyst for the sponsorship package, by coming up with a revolutionary concept of enticing prospective sponsors with an attractive subsidised television advertising campaign.

For Dalton and his small team, the nervous months that followed produced emotions not unlike those an expectant father experiences, as one by one the sponsors committed to the project.

Each negotiation had its own peculiarities, but all took a similar amount of energy and, almost to the day, the process from the first approach to the final 'yes' took exactly three months.

Let's look at how this worked in the case of the ANZ Bank, which was the second sponsor to come aboard.

An unusual feature of the ANZ deal was that it was sold from the middle up, not from the top down, which is a more common occurrence. Grant and his team had learned that unless the CEO wants to be involved in the project, you may as well forget it. With ANZ, the initial approach was made as usual to the CEO, Alister Maitland, who assigned his public relations officer, Mark Scott, to evaluate the proposal.

Every sponsorship proposal needs a champion within the company to make it work, and in this case it was Mark.

He was present at the initial meeting, when Peter Rotgans and Grant showed a video and slides and handed over a painting of *New Zealand Endeavour* sailing with an ANZ spinnaker flying. Then, as the proposal took tentative steps up the corporate ladder, further presentations took place, followed by myriad in-house memos, with Mark Scott working solidly in the background, devising ways in which his bank could benefit from the sponsorship.

The proposal finally made it back to CEO level, and yet another presentation took place. Alister Maitland was all but ready to commit ANZ to the project, but he wanted the endorsement of the bank's board of management in Melbourne.

The final step of the marathon was for Grant and Mark Scott to fly to Melbourne. After making his final pitch to the ANZ board, Grant returned to his hotel while the final decision was made. As he sat watching a movie in his hotel room, the deal was won and lost at least twice inside the space of an hour before the decision went in his favour.

The complexity of the *New Zealand Endeavour* sponsorship deals, and the fact that each was handled on a personal basis, meant that a stronger bond developed between the sponsors and the boat than one would normally expect. Throughout the campaign each of the sponsors' CEOs was ready and willing to talk through any problem. The decision to invest millions of dollars in a Whitbread campaign is a combination of vision and trust. Emotion is also involved, and the people who make these decisions like to stay close to the campaign and remain intimately involved with its progress.

An enormous debt of gratitude is owed to the people who pushed *New Zealand Endeavour*'s barrow within their organisations. People like Brian Aitken and Joe Pope at ENZA; Alister Maitland, Mike O'Neill, Mark Scott and Jonathon Sibley at ANZ; Mike Walshe at BP; George Newton and David Patten at CLEAR; David Bale and

Logos of the seven sponsors of the New Zealand Endeavour *campaign.*

Phil Prosser at the Lotteries Commission; Bob Field and Gary McIver at Toyota; and the late Ken Gray, who saw a way for the Health Sponsorship Council, under the banner of Smokefree, to take its message to a vast audience.

Once the last financial hurdle was crossed, Grant was able to transfer his attention to matters he was more familiar with — organising the design of the new boat and the people who would ultimately race her.

The initial commission for a new Bruce Farr design took place while the search for sponsorship continued at full pace. The choice between a maxi ketch or one of the new Whitbread 60 class boats was far from resolved, however. A study was commissioned by Grant to find out exactly which boat was faster, and a 'race' was simulated on Bruce's computer through the expected weather patterns. The contest that emerged was so close that it was impossible to call a winner.

During the stopover in Fort Lauderdale in the 1989/1990 Whitbread race, the Race Committee announced the new Whitbread 60 class for the following race. At this time, they gave an undertaking to the skippers that the maxis would remain the premier class. With this in mind, Grant now took his computer results to the committee and suggested that the emerging fleet of 60s needed to be slowed down.

To achieve this, a ruling was passed restricting the use of masthead spinnakers on the 60s to only two of the six legs. This effectively reduced their horsepower in the predominantly downwind conditions on the remaining four legs — much to the

The brains behind New Zealand Endeavour's *design: Grant Dalton, Kevin Shoebridge, Bruce Farr, Murray Ross and Russell Bowler.*

dismay of several of the skippers. While the Whitbread 60s wings were clipped, the maxis were allowed to fly gennakers during the race, which was to speed them up considerably.

Farr ran the revised numbers through his computer, and the maxis emerged with a 120-hour advantage around the world. This computer-generated conjecture was enough to give Grant Dalton the confidence to make the decision to build a ketch for the upcoming race.

Ironically, Grant shared expenses in the embryonic research and development programme with two of his main competitors, Daniel Mallé (*La Poste*) and the perennial Pierre Fehlman (*Merit Cup*). This may seem a little strange considering the intense rivalry between the campaigns, but it did save costs in the early design process and during tank testing. While Bruce has a happy knack of being able to 'run with the hares and hunt with the hounds', without anyone questioning his integrity, you are at his mercy when it comes to how your boat compares in size and performance against your competitors. Because the design is based on the weather data that each syndicate provides, Bruce can come back with, 'Well, it is the fastest boat I could design for you in the weather model you provided,' if the boat does not perform as you hoped.

Nothing beats experience, and with this in mind Grant approached Murray Ross and Kevin Shoebridge to join him in the *New Zealand Endeavour* campaign. Murray was Grant's navigator and second in command on board *Fisher and Paykel* and, with his enormous wealth of yacht racing experience, was able to contribute greatly in the design phase of the project. Kevin had raced in the previous two Whitbreads and had recently returned from the America's Cup in San Diego.

Drawing on the valuable lessons learned in the last Whitbread race, Grant, Kevin and Murray were able to come up with a number of ideas as to what sort of boat they wanted Bruce Farr to design.

In addition to 'gut feeling', Farr needed to know in what type of weather conditions the boat was expected to be strongest. In the previous Whitbread, *Fisher and Paykel* revealed a crippling Achilles heel in light winds, so Grant was adamant that, if nothing else, his new boat would be quick in these light to moderate conditions, which, historically, predominate in the Whitbread.

The maxi ketches are designed under the IOR (International Offshore Rule), which, while being in some ways a little antiquated, does produce very even boats and close racing. Designers can, however, juggle with the various dimensions of the boat to suit various wind conditions.

The formula that the top international naval architects such as Bruce Farr use to design these boats is enough to give most people a serious migraine just looking at the multitude of figures. In the not-too-distant past, yacht designers would build a scale half-model of a hull out of a block of wood to a shape that suited their practised eye. Now yachts are designed with the aid of very powerful computers. Equipped with the requirements and parameters that Grant, Kevin and Murray had provided,

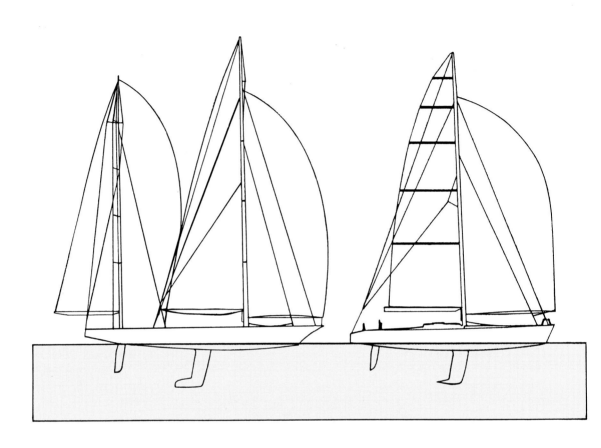

MAXI KETCH VS. WHITBREAD 60

	MAXI KETCH	WHITBREAD 60
Length overall	85 ft 0 in 25.90 m	64 ft 0 in 19.50 m
Water line length	65 ft 7 in 20.00 m	60 ft 0 in 18.00 m
Beam	19 ft 7 in 6.00 m	17 ft 3 in 5.25 m
Draft	11 ft 9 in 3.6 m	12 ft 3 in 3.75 m
Weight	61,064 lb 27,700 kg	33,068 lb 13,500 kg
Water Ballast	None	11,022 lb 5,000 kg
Sail Area – upwind	5,000 sq ft 464 sq m	2,400 sq ft 220 sq m
Sail Area – downwind	8,500 sq ft 789 sq m	4,488 sq ft 417 sq m
Construction	Carbon/Kevlar Nomex/foam	Kevlar/foam
Number of crew	14–16	10–12

Farr set about converting concepts into something that the boat builders could work with.

The first step in this sequence of events is to make a decision on the basic dimensions of the boat, including its length, width, draft, displacement and rig.

The primary difference between *New Zealand Endeavour* and more conventional yachts, including the Whitbread 60 class, is that she is a ketch — a vessel with two masts, the forward being the tallest. The Whitbread is largely a downwind race, with the wind predominantly coming from the side or behind the boat. Such conditions are perfect for a ketch, as the clouds of sail that can be set on the mizzen mast generate a massive amount of power, particularly in light winds. The Whitbread 60s trump card was their ability to carry water ballast, which added great stability and, consequently, increased speed.

The IOR provides mizzen sail area 'cheaply' within its complex formula, which is the primary reason for this new generation of maxi ketches having much bigger mizzen masts than *Steinlager 2* or *Fisher and Paykel*. To take full advantage of this bonus in the rule, Murray, Grant and Kevin were keen to have *New Zealand Endeavour*'s mizzen mast the same height as the main mast. Bruce Farr was less enamoured with this radical idea. He was concerned that the boat's handling characteristics and the engineering nightmare of designing such a huge mizzen mast would make it impractical. Under sufferance, he eventually agreed to design the boat with a mizzen mast some two metres shorter than the main mast — still a considerable advance on the previous generation of ketches.

With the basic boat now designed, Grant and his lieutenants began to plan the deck and interior layout. Based on their experience and personal preferences, they sought the most efficient and lightest options. As is the case with most grant prix race boats, weight was the ultimate consideration, in designing a very simple interior. There would be no sitting around a table; the wet sails would serve that purpose. Our cook, Cole Sheehan, would make do with four gas burners, gimballing in a light (but very expensive) titanium frame. It was decided to leave the interior of the boat unpainted, opting for the bare black carbon-fibre surface. While this saved in excess of 100 kilograms, it recreated the ambience of the Black Hole of Calcutta.

Once Bruce and his design engineer, Russell Bowler, had completed the design to their exacting standards, it was ready to be transformed from megabytes of computer data that had been tested on electronic oceans into a hi-tech boat in which we could blast across the wet stuff.

Grant had formed a good relationship with Auckland boat builder Steve Marten during *Fisher and Paykel*'s construction, so he decided to have his new pride and joy built at the same Pakuranga yard. Steve and his team were responsible for the construction of the America's Cup yachts, *KZ 7*, *NZL 20* and the enormous *K* boat, in addition to *Fisher and Paykel*, and were experienced in the use of state-of-the-art materials.

New Zealand Endeavour's life began as a wooden mould built from huge mylar templates generated on Bruce Farr's computer. This mould was covered in layers of expensive black carbon fibre and golden-coloured Kevlar cloth. Throughout the laminating process, dozens of boat builders resembled a swarm of bees, as they lay suspended on framing above the mould, applying the cloth with careful precision. At various stages of construction, the mould was wheeled into a huge oven, where computers carefully monitored the temperature and humidity while the epoxy-resin-impregnated cloth was 'cooked' to full strength. In between the two carbon and Kevlar skins of the hull was a combination of Nomex honeycomb and high-density foam core. The total hull and deck weight for the 85-foot-long boat was a mere 1,800 kilograms, incredibly light for a structure so strong.

While Kevin Shoebridge concentrated on the hull and deck detailing, Glen Sowry (who joined the crew as a watch captain) worked in the small office at Marten Marine, looking after the initial electronic specifications and ordering the safety equipment the boat was required to carry. Having raced together in the previous two Whitbread races, the pair found this an easy alliance and many hours were spent brainstorming

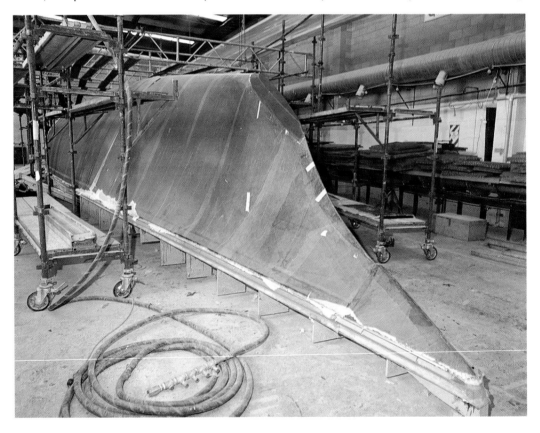

The radical clipper bow begins to take shape after the first layer of carbon fibre has been applied to the mould.

and developing concepts. The remaining members of the core group of *New Zealand Endeavour's* crew were busy drawing together the other components that would enable the boat to become a living, breathing thing as soon as it left the boat builder's shed.

Murray Ross was assigned the task of organising the all-important sail inventory. In previous campaigns of this magnitude, it has not been uncommon to have all the sails built by just one sail loft. While this ensures continuity, it does make for somewhat tunnelled vision. During the closing stages of the Fastnet race four weeks before the start of the last Whitbread, it became abundantly clear to the *Fisher and Paykel* crew that their spinnakers and gennakers were woefully off the pace when they were run down by *Steinlager 2*. The problem was remedied by having new spinnakers built by the English Banks Sails loft. With these, *Fisher and Paykel* was significantly more competitive. It was not surprising, then, that Grant and Murray ordered sails from different sources for the 1993/1994 campaign.

All the 'working sails' — the mainsails, mizzens, genoas and mizzen staysails — were made from Kevlar by the Lidgard loft in Auckland. Jim Lidgard and Richard

New Zealand Endeavour *rapidly begins to take shape as the internal bulkheads are fitted.*

McKay have long been building competitive sails from their loft, but have never received the international exposure they deserved.

Tenders for the critically important spinnakers, gennakers and mizzen gennakers were initially shared among three overseas lofts with formidable reputations for producing consistently fast downwind sails: Banks, who had come to *Fisher and Paykel*'s rescue in the last race, and top American lofts Halsey and Sobstad. After extensive testing, both on the Hauraki Gulf and racing around Europe, a decision was made to get the bulk of these sails from Sobstad, with a few from Halsey. Both of these lofts were instrumental in *America 3*'s convincing defence of the last America's Cup in San Diego.

As *New Zealand Endeavour* neared the completion of her construction, two senior members of the crew were busy organising other aspects of the campaign. Allan Prior, who had sailed two legs on board *Fisher and Paykel* in the previous Whitbread, was overseeing the construction of the aluminium rigging at Southern Spars, an Auckland-based company that has earned itself a fine reputation for building fast masts. Allan was also involved in the initial logistics of setting up a shore base on Auckland's Princes Wharf, finding a suitable barge and establishing workshops, offices and a sail loft.

The remaining member of the core crew was Tony Rae, veteran of the previous

The deck is lifted off the mould and rolled upright in preparation for joining to the hull.

two Whitbreads with Glen and Kevin. Appointed as on-board medic, Tony spent many days training with the Taranaki Ambulance Service in New Plymouth under Scott Hollingshead. In between preparing himself for accidents we hoped would never happen, Tony spent time at the McCann Erickson advertising offices, organising for the mould on which *New Zealand Endeavour* was built to be transformed into a full-size replica of the real thing, to accompany us during our Round New Zealand Roadshow tour in the New Year. After several weeks surrounded by advertising people, we began to worry about Tony's sanity; he was starting to eat trendy food and speak a strange language. It was time to pull him back into the 'real' world of yacht racing.

Tony did not have long to wait, as *New Zealand Endeavour* was fast approaching completion. The last of the scheduled seventeen weeks of construction was nothing short of chaotic. Boat builders, engineers, electricians and painters were crawling all over each other in a frenzied rush to ensure our new pride and joy rolled out the door on time. When it all looked impossible with only a day to go, someone waved a magic wand over the gleaming white boat and miraculously she emerged into daylight to be fitted onto her keel and loaded onto a truck for her delivery to the sea.

For Grant, what had sometimes seemed like impossibly long odds evaporated, as the result of months of hassling, coercing and determination sat ready to meet her natural element for the first time. He was back in business.

New Zealand Endeavour *gets her feet wet for the first time.*

CHAPTER TWO

Back in Business

New Zealand Endeavour finally got her feet wet on 28 October, with a minimum of fuss and ceremony at the Devonport Naval Dockyard. A high-profile naming ceremony was set to take place in Wellington a little over a week away, so there was no need to make too big a deal out of her inaugural splash. Having made her first trip across the sea on the deck of a barge from Half Moon Bay to the dockyard, *New Zealand Endeavour* was then carefully lifted into the Waitemata by the huge floating crane *Hikinui*. After the only formality of the day, a blessing from the Navy Chaplain, we prepared to motor our new pride and joy back across the harbour to our shore base at Princes Wharf.

As Grant took the helm for the first time and we slipped the dock lines for the short journey across the harbour, a near-disaster occurred. A feature of many racing boats such as *New Zealand Endeavour* is a delicate hi-tech, propeller drive system, with shear pins built in to protect it from damage. We very nearly damaged a lot more than the drive when one of the pins sheared and the boat began drifting at an alarming rate in the swift outgoing tide towards the concrete wharf.

Fortunately, prior to casting off the dock lines we had attached a line to our inflatable chaseboat as a precaution against just such a mishap. Before the chaseboat reached full throttle and the line took effect, visions of the sleek white hull of his new multi-million-dollar boat being smashed against the wharf flashed through Grant's mind. After this anxious heart flutter, the remainder of *New Zealand Endeavour's* maiden voyage passed uneventfully.

Once the towering masts had been stepped into the boat, tongues were soon wagging around the waterfront. No one had seen a maxi ketch with such a huge mizzen mast. Many hours were spent tuning the new rigs under the watchful eye of their designer, Steve Wilson. If any one of the spider's web of slender rods were to fail or become unbalanced with respect to the other rods, the result would be an expensive lump of scrap metal lying in the water.

After only two days of commissioning and sea trials, we left Auckland for *New Zealand Endeavour's* first real test, a sail around North Cape and down the west coast of the North Island to Wellington for the naming ceremony. For the first day or two, we took it easy as we became familiar with the boat's complex systems. No matter how experienced a crew is, it always takes time to find your way around the maze of different-coloured ropes snaking all over the deck.

It was not long before the first problem was revealed. To save weight in the boat, a decision had been made to build the engine and generator exhaust system from carbon fibre, instead of the more conventional and much heavier rubber hose. The only drawback of the carbon exhaust, as we were soon to discover, was a potential

New Zealand Endeavour *stretches her legs for the first time on the Hauraki Gulf.*

for leaks. A few tiny pin holes, the result of not enough resin in the laminate, were discovered as water escaped the ducting into the back of the navigation station and some of the electronic equipment. Because we could not motor, we were becalmed for several hours in an unusually tranquil Cook Strait. With a tight deadline to meet in Wellington, a temporary exhaust system was rigged up. The only hose we could find that was big enough was the head fan ducting. Faced with the predicament of no motor, the prospect of foul air trapped in the head did not seem such a big deal.

A few eyebrows had been raised in Auckland when Grant announced that *New Zealand Endeavour* would be launched in Wellington. In previous major campaigns, be they Whitbread or America's Cup, Auckland had always assumed 'ownership', as the boats are normally based in the City of Sails and, in the case of the Whitbread, the race stops there. However, one of the ideas behind the *New Zealand Endeavour* project was to decentralise the campaign from Auckland and involve as many New Zealanders as possible. By christening the boat in Wellington, Grant and his marketing team hoped to eliminate some of the 'us and them' syndrome. The fact that six of the

Lowering the big mizzen staysails required plenty of teamwork.

seven sponsors had their head offices in the capital was also a major consideration.

Steinlager 2 started a trend with night-time christening ceremonies, and we were to take it a step further, with a spectacular event taking place in front of Sir Frank Kitts Park, right in the centre of the city. Amidst a display of fireworks, singing and Maori action songs, New Zealand's golden girl at the Barcelona Olympics, Barbara Kendall, had the honour of breaking the customary bottle of France's finest over the radical clipper bow. The decision to hold the event in Wellington was fully justified, as citizens in their thousands packed the foreshore and the harbour to watch Barbara do her best to break *New Zealand Endeavour*'s bow off with the champagne bottle. The launching was shown live on Television New Zealand, an endorsement of the commitment they had made to the campaign.

As part of the weekend's festivities, *New Zealand Endeavour* competed in her first race the following day in very light conditions around Wellington Harbour. The

New Zealand Endeavour, *the star of a spectacular launching ceremony.*

handicappers had severely misjudged the speed a maxi is capable of in very light airs and we flew around the course for an easy win.

With the formalities over, we set sail for Auckland, this time up the east coast, to complete our circumnavigation of the North Island. A bumpy ride was in store as we rounded Cape Palliser for a 350-mile beat to East Cape into a strong northerly wind — definitely not what was needed after a few days of serious partying. The homeward stretch from East Cape across to Auckland gave *Endeavour* her first opportunity to show us what she was capable of. It quickly became apparent that this new generation of ketches was significantly quicker than its predecessors, as we blasted across the Bay of Plenty and the Hauraki Gulf under a combination of spinnakers and gennakers.

Back at base, we began to tackle the large work list that had been compiled during the trip to Wellington. As with any new boat, there were numerous teething problems that had to be corrected, and we had only four weeks before we sailed across the Tasman for the Sydney to Hobart race.

In an attempt to generate more interest in this event, Kodak put up a prize of $A100,000 to the first boat to break the seventeen-year-old race record, held by the American ketch *Kialoa III*. Before we knew what was going on, *Endeavour* was the centre of intense media speculation as to whether the record could be broken. To stir things up even more, some of the Australian owners were kicking up a fuss about the new Kiwi 'super boat' coming across the Tasman to steal their race off them.

The host club of the Sydney to Hobart is the Cruising Yacht Club of Australia, nestled on the shores of Rushcutters Bay. Many Australian yachting legends have been nurtured in the hallowed bars of the CYCA over vast quantities of Foster's. We were soon to discover that our shore crew rigger, Kevin Batten, who had lived and worked in Sydney, was a bit of a 'ledgie'. Many Aussie yachties, resplendent with zinc-covered noses, could be heard singing Kevin's praises in the bar as yet another schooner of the amber nectar slid down their throats. Less popular with the catering staff at the club was our cook, Cole Sheehan, who decided late one evening that the boys looked a bit hungry and proceeded to pour 200 sausages out of a container onto the barbecue. Cole's normal culinary flair was absent by this stage of the evening and he successfully burnt the whole lot, much to the resident chef's chagrin.

The start of the Sydney to Hobart is probably the only event in the world to rival Auckland at the restart of the Whitbread in sheer numbers of spectators both on and off the water. We were anxious to avoid any potential collisions or drama getting out through Sydney Heads, so made the decision to start conservatively. This approach saw us relegated to the second row at the start, as we also misjudged the critical time-on-distance run for the line. By the time we cleared Sydney Heads in fifth place, the parochial Australian television commentators had counted us out of the race, claiming that *New Zealand Endeavour* was not all she was hyped up to be.

Within an hour of clearing the Heads, those same commentators were eating humble pie, as the big white Kiwi ketch stretched her legs and quickly overtook the

leading boats as they reached down the New South Wales coast towards Bass Strait. However, any hopes we may have entertained about breaking *Kialoa III*'s record rapidly diminished as we sat becalmed for several hours during the first night. When the breeze finally did filter in, *New Zealand Endeavour* was able to display her awesome light-air speed and we dropped the second-placed Australian pocket maxi *Amazon* back over the horizon.

At the pre-race briefing, Grant and Murray had been warned to expect very changeable conditions, and the forecasters' predictions were borne out when, on the second night, one of the area's infamous 'southerly busters' careered across Bass Strait, clobbering us with its full force. The front's abrupt arrival was to be the first real test of the boat and the crew's mettle. Pitch-black skies and gale-driven rain made life difficult for the helmsman, as he struggled to keep his eyes focused in the darkness while spectacular lightning bolts flashed all around us. Our masts were the only

Within a few hours of the start, the opposition are already on the horizon astern of us as we close reach down the New South Wales coast.

potential targets for these, and stories of yachts' whole electrical systems being destroyed by a lightning strike made for a few anxious hours.

With the worst of the southerly front past us, we were left to contend with strong headwinds. *New Zealand Endeavour* was proving to be a bit too tender, the yachtsman's description of a boat not having sufficient stability. The result of this is that the boat cannot carry as much sail as she should. It is all very well having a big boat with a lot of sail, but if she cannot handle the power the sails produce, she is not extracting her maximum speed potential. It is in these conditions that the Whitbread 60s, with their water ballasting capabilities, would have a strong edge on us.

Even with the park-up we had experienced in the early stages of the race and the gale slowing our progress towards Hobart, we still had an outside chance of breaking the record as we surged along Tasmania's east coat. Until, that is, the breeze gave us another slap in the face by all but dying right away and then coming ahead of us to make progress frustratingly slow. *New Zealand Endeavour* drifted up the notoriously fickle Derwent River into the heart of Hobart with a comfortable lead of three hours and 22 minutes over *Amazon*. Even with the unsuitable conditions, we had posted the third-fastest time on record – not too bad for the boat's first major race.

Initially it had looked as if *Endeavour* might pull off the double — winning both line honours and on corrected time. But as the breeze increased, so did the smaller boats' prospects, and the irrepressible Syd Fisher beat us for corrected-time honours in his Farr 50 *Ragamuffin*. After twenty attempts at winning the Sydney to Hobart, Fisher had finally achieved his goal.

Hobart is famous for its hospitality at the end of the 630-mile race and, in keeping with tradition, we did our best to enjoy the festivities. After indulging in large quantities of the local delicacy, scallop pies, and Cascade lager, we were ready for a long sleep. Incidentally, an unusual phenomenon often afflicts yachtsmen visiting Hobart. Known as 'Cascades throat', it has the effect of anaesthetising the vocal cords making the sufferer sound like the raspy rock star Joe Cocker.

After three days of Tassie hospitality, we prepared to sail up to Melbourne. While it would be fun to spend more time relaxing in port, the clock was always ticking away towards the start of the Whitbread and we had to make the most of every day to improve *Endeavour*'s performance.

On this trip we carried a few representatives of the sponsors on board and they were to get a taste of what life on board a Whitbread boat really is like. Any misconceptions they may have harboured about ocean racing soon dissipated as we bashed our way to windward in strong winds around the west coast of Tasmania.

While we were in Melbourne, Murray fell victim to a spinal injury caused by bumping his head on an exposed winch-drive shaft in the yacht's interior. He flew back to Auckland for treatment and Allan Prior was moved into the navigator's position to get us back to Bluff, at the bottom of the South Island, with Kevin Batten taking his place on deck.

This trans-Tasman trip would take us down into the latitudes that are effectively the top of the Southern Ocean and considerably less hospitable than the Tasman Sea. The predominant westerlies that sweep around the world at these lower latitudes are what make the Whitbread race a supreme challenge and provide the roller-coaster rides that keep us coming back for more. We were hoping to encounter these conditions on the trip to Bluff and were not disappointed.

No sooner had we left the confines of Bass Strait and poked our bow out into the Tasman Sea, then we picked up ever-increasing westerlies. With all the sail set that we could carry at any one time on main and mizzen rigs, we were off down confused seas at breakneck speed. Both *Steinlager 2* and *Fisher and Paykel* had very definite limits as to how much sail they could carry as the wind increased. For the veterans of those boats, *New Zealand Endeavour*'s ability to employ considerably more sail as the wind increased took a lot of getting used to.

Amidst our race-winning celebrations in Hobart, Tony hijacks a local youngster's Sabot to hone up on his dinghy sailing skills.

Not only could our new boat carry more sail, we were soon to discover that to sail the boat to its full potential, we had to fly every square metre of straining spinnaker cloth we could handle to meet the boats VPPs. These are the computer-generated theoretical Velocity Performance Prediction figures, which to most people are no more than a bunch of meaningless numbers. To us, however, they were *Endeavour's* life blood, The VPPs were constantly being updated to reflect the true speed the boat was capable of. At sea in the middle of a cold and miserable night, it is very easy to say, 'The boat is going just fine,' when in reality it may be sailing at a critical fraction of a knot slower than it should be. The VPPs reminded us that we had to avoid lulling ourselves into a false sense of security and, instead, should continue pushing the boat or ourselves to the maximum potential.

Keeping *Endeavour* at full speed through the desolate stretches of Southern Ocean in the months ahead was going to ensure a continuing source of grey hair or, in Grant's case, the end of what hair he had remaining. In 35 knots of wind, most boats are becoming unmanageable under spinnaker. Not only was our new sled still on the rails in these conditions, we were flying a veritable cloud of sail. When the big mizzen gennaker set in this much wind with a thundering crack, the sensation was not unlike a turbo booster cutting in on a high-performance car. The sudden increase in acceleration as the boat leapt forward could very quickly have terminal consequences if the helmsman or trimmer were caught napping.

As well as giving the boat a work-out and finding what she was capable of in these rugged conditions, the trip to Bluff was a perfect opportunity to give the human cargo a taste of what was to come. Steering any big boat at these speeds with the throttles opened right out is both physically and mentally demanding, requiring helmsmen with a rare aptitude. This had been the principle that Grant had subscribed to from day one, as he began to select and recruit his crew. It is no good having only a handful of good drivers; in order to win, we would need every crew member to steer the boat well in all conditions.

For some of the younger guys, like Mike Sanderson and Sean Clarkson, their first experience driving a fully powered-up maxi ketch down big breaking seas at these high speeds was a fine balance between blood-pumping adrenalin and total terror. However, as Grant had hoped, all of the new boys on board acquitted themselves well during their first introduction into the high-stress world of Southern Ocean sailing.

During the trip across the Tasman Sea we had clocked up some impressive daily mileages. Our best run was a scorching 375 miles in a twenty-four-hour period, fifteen better than *Steinlager 2* achieved during the last Whitbread race. To blast across the Tasman from the east coast of Tasmania to the west coast of the South Island in a little over two and a half days is the nautical equivalent of low level flying.

As we stormed back home, enjoying a relatively comfortable ride, we could not help but think of the ten crews competing in the British Steel Challenge. These crews were all amateurs, paying $45,000 for the privilege of racing around the world

the wrong way — against the prevailing westerly wind. Our paths must have almost crossed — as we were screaming down the seas towards Bluff, they were bashing their way towards Hobart for the finish of the second leg of their race.

Fifty-five knots of westerly gale blew us into New Zealand's southern-most port, Bluff. This was to be the springboard for the Round New Zealand Roadshow, which, during the following six weeks would visit every major port on New Zealand's lengthy coastline. It would provide the seven sponsors with their biggest opportunity to date to generate publicity and for the campaign to achieve a nationwide profile. The logistics of keeping this ambitious travelling show on schedule and, as importantly, on budget were mind-boggling. The star of the circus was the 85-foot mould on which *New Zealand Endeavour* was built and had subsequently been transformed into a full-size replica. This was broken down into three pieces each time it was transported between towns on army trucks, accompanied by three container-loads of sponsors' displays and marquees.

In contrast to the round the country tours embarked on by previous Whitbread campaigns, the *Endeavour* sponsors worked hard to involve as many people as they could with hands-on displays. Each had a theme that kept people amused — grinding competitions or racing radio-controlled cars around a mini-Whitbread course. The

Foveaux Strait welcomes us back to New Zealand with a 55-knot gale.

boat, too, was always present, allowing the sponsors to invite guests to look over it or go for a short sail around the harbour.

As the replica and the fifty people that manned the sponsors' stands drove in convoy to the next port, we would sail *New Zealand Endeavour* up to meet them. On each leg we sailed with the crew split in half to make room for one representative from each sponsor to join us. During our voyage around the South Island, we encountered particularly rough weather, making for some bumpy rides. As each guest came on board for the over-night sail, we would quietly place odds on who was most likely to lose their dinner.

On one such occasion, as we left Otago Harbour, one of the guests was busy scoffing left-over pork chops and indulging in a few rum and cokes. When we suggested that, based on the weather forecast, it may not be such a good idea to have another drink, he replied, 'Don't worry about me, this is the experience of a lifetime.' Within minutes of heading into the rough open sea, the unfortunate guest was experiencing an altogether different sensation, as he proceeded to return his gastronomic intake to the environment.

Another guest suffering from the less-than-idyllic conditions was bunkbound as we bashed our way to windward in a 40-knot gale. Glen was catching up on some sleep on the sails piled up in the companionway when the 120-kilo guest rolled out of his bunk, crashing down directly on top of the crew member and elbowing him in the face in the process. Hearing the commotion, Allan leaned out of the navigation station and was incapacitated with laughter at the sight of the squashed Glen.

Seeing double: the replica and the real Endeavour *during the Round New Zealand roadshow tour.*

Not too many of the crew would have made good doctors; most of them had the bedside manner of Jack the Ripper whenever one of the guests was ill. Fortunately, Tony Rae and his medical mentor Scott Hollingshead, known as Scott Horrorhead by the crew, were somewhat more sympathetic. But even Tony's good nature was tested one evening when he clambered down through the hatch to find a very green-looking inductee into the world of offshore sailing sitting on the edge of a bunk. A concerned Tony asked, 'Are you going to be sick?' and a polite reply was forthcoming: 'Yes, I think I am.' Suddenly the guest threw up into the only nearby container — Tony's hat.

Once back in Auckland at the completion of the Round New Zealand tour, it was time to take off our PR hats and resume the business of preparing *New Zealand Endeavour* for her imminent trip to Europe. Based on the lessons we learnt in the Hobart race, extra lead was added to the bulb on the bottom of the keel to increase the boat's stability. It is often hard to test the differences that a change like this can make, but the increased stability did seem to make the boat more powerful, an important attribute for a boat that would have to reach across the wind fast in the Whitbread.

In the early stages of the campaign, it had been decided that *New Zealand Endeavour* would compete in the New York to Southampton race in July. We revised this plan when we discovered that our main Whitbread opposition were planning to race in the UAP Round Europe event. The chance to assess the competition was too important to miss, and so *Endeavour* was shipped to Europe.

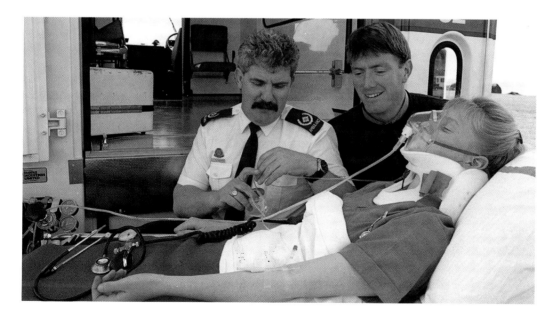

Tony spent many hours with his medical mentor Scott Hollingshead practising for an accident we hoped would never happen.

The intensity of preparation increased during the last few weeks in Auckland. It was going to be a lot easier and cheaper to get things done on the boat in New Zealand than in an unfamiliar country. Meeting us in each stopover during the Whitbread would be containers that would double as workshops and storage. We had to ensure that these were provisioned with all of the spare parts we would need throughout the race and also most of the freeze-dried food that Cole would load on board during each stop-over.

With the boat loaded on board the container ship bound for Europe, our focus changed for the remaining weeks before we flew to England. Throughout our preparations in Auckland, we trained at the Les Mills gym in downtown Auckland under the watchful eye of former Commonwealth Games weight-lifting gold medallist Tony Ebert. Tony had trained the *Fisher and Paykel* crew for the last Whitbread and, with the experience gained from that campaign, was able to put together an excellent programme for us. Immensely popular with the crew, Mighty Mouse was one of those people you just could not put down. If he fell into a sewer, he would probably come up with a smile on his face expounding the virtues of the experience. While Tony was right at home in the gym, he was a veritable fish out of water when it came to refereeing our in house games of touch rugby. Often on the receiving end of some barbed comment from one of the guys as to his refereeing prowess, he seemed to base his decisions on whoever looked the most indignant.

In the *Fisher and Paykel* days, Grant and Tony had put a lot of emphasis on power and strength in the crew. However, to win the Whitbread you need crew that

'I hope that crane driver knows what he's doing!'

are very good yachtsmen first and super athletes second. With this principle firmly in mind, Tony toned down the heavy lifting and concentrated more on the need for more well-rounded aerobic fitness. Strength is obviously needed to handle the heavy sails and gear typical of a maxi, but fitness is what prevents a person from becoming tired, particularly in an endurance event like the Whitbread. After a tough sail change in the middle of the night, it is easy to back off and have a rest instead of staying focused on keeping the boat at full speed, a trap that a fit person is less likely to fall prey to.

With the boat due to arrive in the London port of Tilbury, it was time for the team to pack their bags. Everyone flew up in different stages to meet the boat, with the last group leaving Auckland after the boat had already arrived in our English base of Gosport. Missing was Colin Booth, who had decided to pull out of the crew for personal reasons. The first that most of us knew of his decision was when he did not turn up at the airport. Grant learnt of Colin's decision from Tony Ebert, and to this day we have no idea what really was the cause of his absence. The rest of the team remained, however, firmly committed to the campaign and were looking forward to being reunited with *New Zealand Endeavour*.

New Zealand Endeavour, *sheathed in plastic, sits on the ship that will take her to England.*

33

CHAPTER THREE

Team Endeavour

The *New Zealand Endeavour* team consisted of more than the fourteen men who sailed the boat around the world. It included a seven-member shore crew who followed the yacht to each stopover to prepare it for the next leg of the race. When selecting the team that would race and maintain *New Zealand Endeavour* in the Whitbread race, Grant Dalton looked for some key qualities that are critical for success — ability, commitment, enthusiasm and compatibility. There is no point having a mega rock-star on the boat if they cannot work alongside everyone else as a team player.

In previous Whitbread races, there has been an emphasis on picking crew with 'all-round' skills. The level of competition now apparent in the race demands the need for specialist helmsmen and trimmers. Anyone can learn to change sails or work the halyards in the pit, but the ability to steer and trim a boat well is developed from many years of experience. Almost invariably, the best helmsmen and trimmers learn their craft in the cockpit of a high-performance dinghy, and most of *Endeavour*'s crew were products of this background.

When at sea, there is no shore crew to call on to repair or maintain the yacht's complex equipment, so the sailors must have a few additional arrows in their quiver. Between us on *Endeavour*, we were able to maintain the engines, sails, electronics, hydraulics, rigging and the scores of other systems that make up a high-tech yacht. Ultimately, the crew was a mix of enthusiastic but highly skilled young guys amidst a core team of Whitbread veterans. Eight of the crew had sailed in previous Whitbreads, accumulating twenty-two around-the-world marathons between us. Combined with America's Cup, Admiral's Cup, world championships and just about every ocean race in the world, the *New Zealand Endeavour* crew were arguably the most experienced in the Whitbread race.

Just as important as the sailing crew was our shore team. Some people believe that these guys get the bum end of the deal while the sailors have all the fun and glory. In truth, the shore crew were all very happy with their lot and, as George Jackich succinctly put it, they were happiest when they cast *Endeavour*'s dock lines off and waved us goodbye at the start of each leg. While the sailing crew would arrive in port with stories of life on the high seas, the shore crew would arrive discussing whether they'd enjoyed the in-flight movie or not!

Over the eighteen months that the *Endeavour* campaign was at full strength with a team of twenty-one, we gelled into a close-knit team that not only worked well together, we had a lot of fun along the way.

Following are the great bunch of people who made up the *New Zealand Endeavour* team and proved once again that Kiwis are winners.

Teamwork is an essential ingredient for a successful Whitbread campaign.

Grant Dalton

NICKNAME:	DALTS
AGE:	36
POSITION:	SKIPPER

THE CREW'S VIEW

It was widely believed by the crew that Dalts was a reincarnated Howard Hughes, such was his fetish for cleanliness on the boat. We must have gone close to exhausting the worldwide supply of Jif washing *Endeavour*'s decks.

Considering that in years not too long ago Dalts displayed a remarkable aptitude when it came to drinking alcohol and performing like a trained seal, there has been a close to complete transformation into a teetotaller so seriously did he take his job. At the final crew party in Southampton, it was with some relief that we witnessed Dalts attempting to drink a rum and Coke while standing on his head. He had not forgotten this finely honed skill.

Dalts lead by example and was always in the thick of any action on board. Widely respected by the crew, his fierce competitiveness and drive were major strengths.

Mike Sanderson

NICKNAME:	MOOSE
AGE:	22
POSITION:	TRIMMER

THE SKIPPER'S VIEW

The youngest member of the sailing team, Moose impressed me during the job interview with his self-confidence and desire to do the race. He developed into a talented helmsman and trimmer who never tired of looking up the leech of a genoa or at the luff of a spinnaker for hours on end. As one of only two crew members who hadn't crossed the equator, he was dealt with very severely on that auspicious occasion.

That Moose — twenty-one years old when he joined us — had a house and a steady girlfriend amazed us — he was in fact just as bent as the rest of the crew. He was a trendsetter in the sunglasses world and seemed to have his own sponsorship deal with Oakley, who supplied him with weird-shaped shades on almost every leg.

Allan Prior

NICKNAME: TREV
AGE: 40
POSITION: PITMAN

THE SKIPPER'S VIEW

Not as old as Lowlife, but almost, Trev was a member of the old guard and did his first ocean race before Moose was even born. Although a Kiwi, Trev seems happier in the big US of A, and the whole team spent two years attempting to cure his American speech impediment. In Trev's dialect, Tuesday is said 'Toosday', Newport (where he owns a house) is said 'Nooport' and so it went on.

I wouldn't have been surprised if Trev found the going fairly tough at times; a forty-year-old body, that has been fed huge quantities of amber liquid over the years, has trouble keeping up with a guy in his early twenties. During the UAP Round Europe race I called on him to navigate. With no knowledge of the area and with little time to prepare, he accepted willingly and did an admirable job. It was ultimately his skill that helped us to victory in this very important race.

Sean Clarkeson

AGE: 23
POSITION: BOWMAN

THE SKIPPER'S VIEW

The only team member who never really ended up with a nickname, and who had been to more schools in his childhood than the rest of the team combined. He'd also done everything, from driving trucks in Australia to a couple of years of studying marine biology. His immense strength was only one of his attributes and, having been thrown into the bowman role on my watch, performed with full gusto.

He was perhaps the keenest of all the applicants to do the Whitbread, and even threatened to pull my head off if I didn't take him. That clinched it for him.

Sean suffers from a peculiar Whitbread disease — hair loss —and things don't look good for him by the time the next race comes around in September 1997.

Glen Sowry

NICKNAME: FOXY
AGE: 31
POSITION: WATCH CAPTAIN

THE SKIPPER'S VIEW

Two vivid memories of Foxy will last in the minds of the *Endeavour* team. The first was the day he scaled the mizzen shroud to attach a sheet to a staysail and slid back down, impaling himself on a stanchion. The second was his driving a golf ball off the dock in Gosport into Portsmouth Harbour. Unfortunately, the ball hit a pole, bounced back and struck Foxy in the chin, which split open spectacularly. On both occasions we were laughing too hard to render assistance.

Foxy took the broach that cost us our mizzen very personally, as he was at the helm at the time. The truth is that he was driving because he was probably the boat's best helmsman and it was just one of those things. Maybe we had all got a little complacent at that time and were brought back to reality with a hell of a thump. Another fine team player, Foxy drove himself and his watch very hard.

Nick Willetts

NICKNAME: NUGSIE
AGE: 31
POSITION: TRIMMER

THE SKIPPER'S VIEW

Nugsie held the distinction of being able to tangle almost any sheet lead during a sail change, which meant he ended up wetter than the rest of us as he sorted things out on the leeward rail. At one stage the team considered calling him 'Tangles', but he obviously was able to redeem himself because this name didn't stick.

His dress sense left a little to be desired, typified by cutting the legs off his wet-weather gear trousers to create dungarees. Luckily for him, we had no more bad weather for the rest of that leg.

Before he joined *New Zealand Endeavour*, Nugsie had done just about everything else there was to do in keelboat racing, and now he has a Whitbread under his belt, he's done the lot. He threw himself into his work with dedication and enthusiasm, fitted in quickly and was universally liked.

Stuart Bannatyne

NICKNAME: HERMIE
AGE: 22
POSITION: PITMAN

THE SKIPPER'S VIEW

Employed just prior to the Whitbread, Hermie faced his first trial in the Fastnet. To ensure he didn't make any mistakes that could jeopardise his chances, he asked Shoebie what were the 'do's and don'ts'. Shoebie advised him that getting drunk at the end of the race and making a spectacle of himself would probably be frowned upon. Within two hours of finishing, Hermie had fallen in the water once, and went in twice more before the festivities had concluded. This set the mode for his end-of-leg antics, climaxing in a fall after the finish of the Whitbread that cost him three stitches in his forearm.

Based on his background in Lasers, we always felt he would be a great helmsman and we weren't disappointed. He steered the boat like a master right from the start. Hermie had the opposite problem to Brad, and possibly holds a world record for the least bowel movements over a month. This despite the fact that into his incredibly large mouth he could shovel vast quantities of anything that even resembled food.

David Brooke

NICKNAME: BURT
AGE: 28
POSITION: BOWMAN

THE SKIPPER'S VIEW

Arguably *New Zealand Endeavour*'s best-looking crew member — or so he thought! — Burt spent many hours grooming himself in order to live up to his reputation. Designer stubble, all-over tan, immaculate hair — and enough chat to put even the most interested girl to sleep.

Burt anchored the bow during pre-start manoeuvres and day sailing. He was always willing to go straight up the mast in any weather, preferably with a camera shooting him from the deck. A bowman's job is never easy and is wetter than most. Despite having to do a lot of the grunt work during sail changes, Burt was always laughing in the thick of any manoeuvres.

On the same watch, Burt and Nick would talk non-stop together for hours about nothing, and in lighter winds their voices were capable of keeping the off-watch awake. One of yachting's nice guys, Burt was a very valuable member of the team.

Kevin Shoebridge

NICKNAME: SHOEBIE
AGE: 31
POSITION: WATCH CAPTAIN

THE SKIPPER'S VIEW

Shoebie held the dubious distinction of being *Endeavour*'s shortest crew member. He was also watch captain of the yacht's most unscrupulous watch where thieving chocolate and biscuits was concerned.

Shoebie played a key role in *New Zealand Endeavour*'s success. Involved from the time of design through to building, he was also responsible for the organisation of the team and for turning the yacht around in each port. Despite these responsibilities, he, like most of the team, understood the importance of sponsors and how necessary it was to marry their needs with sailing the boat to its full potential.

Brad Jackson

NICKNAME: SKUNK
AGE: 25
POSITION: TRIMMER

THE SKIPPER'S VIEW

One problem that Skunk had throughout the race was his very smelly 'insides', which could clear the deck or down below of crewmen in seconds. Despite protestations from the rest of the crew to the contrary, Skunk remained adamant that 'chicks loved it'. I have serious doubts about this.

Brad was one of the finds of the trip, turning out to be a superb driver and trimmer, and also a team player who quickly came to grips with the intricacies of living under constant change and pressure. He confessed that one of the highlights of his race had been the development of his golf game. As a natural sportsman, he would frustrate the rest of the crew with the apparent ease at which he could master just about anything he did.

Tony Rae

NICKNAME: TRAE
AGE: 32
POSITION: PIT/MEDIC

THE SKIPPER'S VIEW
At thirty-two years old, Trae still annoys the rest of the team by being ridiculously fit. A team player who just loves being in the thick of things during sail changes. The two days that Trae spent cutting down sails almost non-stop after the mast fell down proved his professionalism and dedication.

Often the boys wondered where Trae and the other sailmakers slipped away to while we were in port. Was it the pub, the beach, endless cups of coffee . . . who will ever know? Nevertheless, the sails were always ready for each leg and our sail programme was ultimately one of the key reasons for our success. Every team needs as many Traes as possible.

Craig Watson

NICKNAME: SPIKE
AGE: 27
POSITION: BOWMAN

THE SKIPPER'S VIEW
Unfortunately for Spike, he made such a good job of being a bowman on *Steinlager 2* that he ended up being quickly slotted into that position on *Endeavour* as well. Every boat needs a 'Mister Fix-it', and Spike was ours. With his engineering background, he ended up looking after the hydraulics, the rigs and all of the rope splicing while we were racing at sea.

Spike became very unpopular during our stay in Gosport before the Whitbread when he started beating all the hot-shot locals with his home-grown model yacht. After a couple of weeks of cleaning up the super-serious locals, he was banned from racing in formal competitions.

It was widely believed among the crew that Spike was probably the world's loudest snorer — sleeping anywhere near him was almost impossible. Such was his aptitude for sleeping while ashore, I often felt that, given half a chance, he would never have turned up for early-morning training at all.

Mike Quilter

NICKNAME: LOWLIFE
AGE: 40
POSITION: NAVIGATOR

THE SKIPPER'S VIEW

Lowlife was the oldest member of the sailing team — he also had a serious chocolate fetish. One should not be fooled by his outwardly laid-back attitude. He is intensely competitive, hard-driving and universally liked by the team. More than a navigator, he spent many hours on deck involved in sail changes to help the yacht's speed.

With an aptitude for computers, he is part of the new breed of racing navigators. Lowlife isn't into taking risks, preferring to work to a predetermined game plan, modified by the vagaries of the weather. Part of the old team on board who first sailed in the Whitbread on *Lion*, along with Dalts, Shoebie, Foxy, Trae and BC.

Cole Sheehan

NICKNAME: BC
AGE: 32
POSITION: COOK/CAMERAMAN

THE SKIPPER'S VIEW

There is not much to say about BC that has not already been said over the years. On looking back to some pictures of him in the *Lion New Zealand* days, it strikes you straight away that in nine years he hasn't aged at all, probably because nothing fazes him. He was constantly under pressure from the boys to stay up at night, but no amount of badgering could ever change his ways. There was even a rumour going around the boat at one stage that BC had accepted a job after the race as a test pilot for Sleepyhead beds.

On his third Whitbread as cook, BC diversified into becoming the on-board cameraman, a job he enjoyed and at which he excelled. We often wondered where he got all his rough-weather footage from, as he was usually absent from the deck once water started pouring over it.

Chris Cooney

Nickname: COOZER
Age: 46
Position: SHORE MANAGER

THE SKIPPER'S VIEW

As the campaign's shore manager, collector of antiques and sporting more suitcases than the average family of five going on a six-month holiday, Coozer had a difficult task controlling the shore-based functions of a multi-million-dollar campaign that changed venue every few weeks. I had spent two campaigns looking for someone who, along with organisational ability, possessed the diplomatic skills to deal with the hundreds of people we come in contact with every day. Chris got it right. He made my life a lot easier, always watching my back and remembering the little things that I would often forget.

George Jackich

Age: 29
Position: SHORE-CREW BOAT BUILDER

THE SKIPPER'S VIEW

When I was trying to track down references on George prior to signing him on, I spoke to Russell Bowler from the Farr office, who had worked with him during the 1992 America's Cup. He said, 'You can't have a campaign without George. Anyone who tells Michael Fay daily that he's in love with him, needs to be involved!'

George is a master with carbon, glue and wood. He's also a dab hand on the guitar and he kept everyone smiling all day. He was a member of a tight-knit and fantastic shore crew who were absolutely pivotal in our victory. Nothing was too much trouble, they never grumbled, always worked hard and made the lives of the sailors' wives easier while travelling.

David Duff

Nickname: DUFFY
Age: 22
Position: SHORE-CREW SAILMAKER

THE SKIPPER'S VIEW

Duffy was subject to fluctuations in his body weight, based on the quantity of liquid he consumed during each stopover, but somehow he always managed to squeeze into his skin-tight jeans. With an infectious laugh, Duffy worked diligently with Trae and Moose at being busy — or certainly looking that way — with the sails in each port. I was often amazed at his recovery rate after a big night out.

The shore-crew sailmaker's job was hotly contested. There were many contenders who had equal skills, but Duffy made it on my perceived feeling that he would be a real team player. I was not disappointed in our youngest member.

Bill Handey

Age: 34
Position: SHORE-CREW ELECTRICIAN

THE SKIPPER'S VIEW

Along with Foxy, Bill was responsible for the electrics both ashore and on board. It was the high-quality maintenance that ultimately gave us a trouble-free system. I believed from the start, that we needed a shore-based electrician, and Bill proved to be just right for the job.

His diligence was not limited to looking after the electrics; Bill could always be counted on to turn on a solid and sometimes spectacular performance when indulging in a few cold ones. Fortunately, when he managed to fall out of a van travelling at great speed through the streets of Punta del Este, he was well anaesthetised.

Kevin Batten

NICKNAME: KEV A
AGE: 27
POSITION: SHORE-CREW RIGGER

THE SKIPPER'S VIEW

Despite the fact that Kev is a true blue Kiwi, he managed to get labelled as an Aussie when he worked for *Spirit of Australia* in the last America's Cup. He was therefore named Kev A, and as far as we could ascertain was something of a legend at the Cruising Yacht Club of Australia.

Organised, hard-working and always happy, the highlight of his campaign was flying the Cathay Pacific 747 jumbo jet during delivery of the spare mizzen mast from England to Australia.

Annie Hodgkinson

AGE: 43
POSITION: SHORE-CREW COOK

THE SKIPPER'S VIEW

Annie had an unenviable task. As shore-based cook she had to cater to the needs of nineteen fussy males, all with different tastes. Added to this, in most cases she was producing meals three times a day in surroundings designed for a family of five.

Like the rest of her shore-crew compatriots, she loved nothing better than a big night out, the only difference being that she would be chasing unsuspecting blokes.

Our meals were first class and, except for the rare occasions when the meat was burnt on the barbecue, no one ever moaned — quite a testimony considering yachting teams usually never stop complaining about the food.

Carol Vincent

THE SKIPPER'S VIEW

My trusted marketing manager started with the campaign long before there was a yacht or crew, and by the end she was the longest-serving team member.

Her responsibilities were as diverse as organising the newsletter and sponsor requests, as overseeing the *New Zealand Endeavour* replica, the Auckland stopover and the roadshow — in short, if it happened in New Zealand and had anything to do with the sponsors or marketing, Carol organised it. Hers was not an easy job when the real action seemed to be on the other side of the world, however, big-time sailing is now a marketing-driven sport, and Carol's contribution was critical.

The New Zealand Endeavour *crew.*

Endeavour *at speed. The reversal of the logos on the asymmetric spinnaker is caused by the sail being turned 'inside out' through a gybe.*

CHAPTER FOUR

Testing Times

There is only so much training you can do before you need to go racing against some serious opposition to check up on both the crew's and boat's performance. In an intensive racing environment you learn more in a couple of weeks than you would in three or four months practising on your own. The UAP Round Europe race was to be the campaign's first real acid test, and it was with an air of keen anticipation that most of the team arrived in England to join the boat.

While the rest of us had been enjoying a break in Auckland, the advance guard of Trev, Spike, Brad, Burt, Kev A, Bill, George and Chris had done a great job of putting *New Zealand Endeavour* back into racing mode at the Tilbury container terminal in London, where it had just arrived after a journey halfway around the world.

With only three days to go before we were due to sail across to France for the start of the Round Europe race, Dalts decided we should have a sail around the Isle of Wight to blow the cobwebs out. Little did we know as we cast off the mooring lines from our marina berth that the next few hours would see major upheaval in the team.

Throughout the early stages of the campaign, Murray Ross had frequently raised concerns about the reliability of some aspects of the electrical system on board *Endeavour*. Since launching, we had experienced power spikes within the system, caused because the charging cables were not wired through the batteries before they went to the switchboard. The batteries effectively act as a filter when wired correctly, so that any voltage spikes are suppressed before any voltage-sensitive electronic equipment can be damaged. By rewiring the cables in this configuration, we eliminated this problem, but there were a few other teething problems with some of the hi-tech instruments in the navigation station.

From the day Murray arrived in England to rejoin the team, everyone sensed that, despite the break we had all just had, he was not happy. The fact that Colin Booth had just left the campaign undoubtedly had some bearing on his attitude, given that Colin is his regular crew in double-handed racing.

The lid blew off the pressure cooker while *New Zealand Endeavour* bashed its way to windward out in the English Channel behind the Isle of Wight. As we bounced off one particularly big wave, a loose battery link broke contact for a split second and the navigation electronics suffered a power interruption. This was the straw that broke the camel's back. Murray immediately called Dalts down to the navigation station for a summit meeting.

Murray explained that he certainly wanted to do the race, but carrying out navigation responsibilities to his high standard was, he felt, becoming difficult. Over the next hour or so, Murray and Grant calmly discussed the problem. They were

The European yachting establishment were very impressed with New Zealand Endeavour*'s deck layout.*

good friends and had experienced the disappointment of chasing *Steinlager 2* around the World four years earlier. However, playing on Dalt's mind was that he felt some of the younger crew members were scared of Murray, who often criticised their performance without giving any constructive advice. While there was an immense amount of talent amongst the new blood, they often felt inhibited to let it flow in case it met with Murray's wrath. Definitely not a healthy environment in which to build a winning team.

On deck, the remainder of the crew continued sailing, oblivious of the drama that was unfolding below. By the time *Endeavour* had turned for the run home up the Solent to Gosport, Grant had reached his decision. He asked Allan Prior if he would navigate the boat around the treacherous European coastline in the upcoming race. Trev stepped in without blinking — a gutsy response given the lack of time he had to prepare for the race. Meanwhile, Dalts discussed the situation with Shoebie and Glen to ensure he had their support. Dalts was anxious not to cut off his nose to spite his face, and so agreed with Murray that he should think about it for a few hours and talk to his long-term sailing partner Colin Booth before making a decision.

Murray laid the blame for the electronics problem on Glen and went on to suggest that Boothy, an auto electrician, should rejoin the crew. For Glen and Bill, the shore-crew electrician, this came as something of a slap in the face. Many of the problems, they felt, were the result of the contractor's installation at the time the boat was being built. They considered that Murray had been too quick to stand back and criticise rather than help to find solutions. Grant, however, was never going to accept Murray's ultimatum, which would not only send the wrong signals about his campaign, but would perhaps be the start of the unravelling of a very long ball of string. He also felt it would mean losing someone who, in his opinion, was just as important as Murray if *New Zealand Endeavour* was to win the Whitbread.

By the time Dalts went to Murray's room to tell him of his final decision, Murray's bags were already packed. Once he had left, there was a perceptible lightening of mood among the team. It was almost as if the black cloud we had been living under had blown away overnight.

Incidents like this seem to be a bigger deal outside the team than they are within it. Like Colin's leaving, it hardly created a ripple among the crew. If Murray was not with us any more, we would find someone else. In fact, a plan for this eventuality had been devised many months before. By the time the boat reached Stockholm at the end of the Round Europe race, the highly experienced and equally popular Mike Quilter had joined us as navigator. It all went to prove that no one person is irreplaceable, or bigger than the team as a whole.

New Zealand Endeavour left a blustery south coast of England the day after Murray's departure, heading for La Rochelle on the Atlantic coast of France. We had already received special dispensation from the race committee to arrive a day later than originally required, so it was throttles open for the sail across the Channel and into the Bay of Biscay to join our competitors.

The weather was determined to give us a ride bumpy enough to be in keeping with the previous few days' events. On the first night out, our ageing Kevlar mainsail ripped as we were reefing it. With a tight timetable to meet and the threat of a hefty financial penalty being incurred, we had to motor sail without our main in order to remain on schedule. We found ourselves running out of fuel as we neared La Rochelle, but our shore crew, with the aid of the *La Poste* chaseboat, came to our rescue and brought out enough diesel to enable us to motor the remaining few miles.

Our main Whitbread rivals, Pierre Fehlman's *Merit Cup* and Daniel Mallé's *La Poste*, were already moored in the small lock in the town centre when we arrived. As we brought *New Zealand Endeavour* alongside, the scene was akin to a couple of boxers eyeing each other before a fight. The European crews were as anxious to see their competitor from Down Under as we were to see their boats. It quickly became evident that *Endeavour*'s deck layout was significantly more simplistic and functional. Many of the French sailing heavies were very impressed with the overall thinking and design of the white boat that had travelled from New Zealand to take them on.

With the exception of New Zealanders, the French are the most enthusiastic followers of yachting in the world. Whenever a boat entered La Rochelle, a huge sound system would blare out suitably dramatic music and a crowd would gather

The big-budget, high-profile La Poste *was competitive in the Round Europe, but fell off the pace once the Whitbread started.*

around the lock entrance to catch a glimpse of the newcomer.

After a day in La Rochelle finalising our preparations and soaking up the atmosphere around the town, it was time to start formulating a game plan for the first leg to Gijon, in northern Spain. It was in the middle of one of these meetings, that an ashen-faced George interrupted to inform Grant that we had a serious structural problem with the boat. While climbing forward inside the boat during a routine check, George had noticed that the hull laminate near the bow was very soft under foot — scarily soft.

The meeting broke up and we all rushed down to the boat to check out George's depressing discovery. While Grant and Shoebie followed a very concerned George into the black cavernous bow, Moose donned scuba gear and soon reported that the outside skin was also fractured. The problem seemed to be that sections of the carbon fibre skin had come unstuck from the Nomex honeycomb core.

Dalts' next few hours were spent on the phone to Russell Bowler at the Farr design office in Annapolis, discussing whether some sort of temporary repair could be made to allow us to start the race. Russell burnt the midnight oil to run some calculations and came back with instructions for George to laminate an extra layer of high-density foam inside the hull to beef up the affected areas. The somewhat alarming recommendation was made to keep an eagle eye on the patch if we encountered any bumpy conditions in the Bay of Biscay, notorious for its big seas and gales.

As it turned out, Huey, the Kiwi yachties' wind god, was smiling on us and we raced across to Gijon in relatively placid conditions. The French fans cheered their compatriots on *La Poste* as they led the fleet out into the ocean, but this enthusiasm was to be short-lived as *New Zealand Endeavour* powered into the lead soon after leaving the confines of the bay. Daniel Mallé's men enjoyed massive support from their sponsors, the French postal service, and it was to be a popular misconception that the crew was made up entirely of French postmen. They were, in fact, mostly top French professional yachtsmen and the closest many had come to being postmen was collecting the mail out of their letter boxes.

As the fleet headed across the Bay of Biscay, it rapidly became apparent that there was very little difference in boat speed between *New Zealand Endeavour* and her European near sister-ships. After a demanding 250-mile leg to Gijon in very changeable conditions, first blood was drawn by Pierre Fehlman's *Merit Cup* by a mere minute and three seconds. As this was our first race since the Sydney to Hobart, five months previously, it was taking us a while to switch back into full competition mode.

Before the start of the Round Europe race, there had been considerable media interest in this inaugural skirmish between the maxi ketches and the Whitbread 60s. As it turned out, the conditions experienced for much of the Europe race favoured the ketches, with predominantly light to moderate winds encouraging vast sail areas.

The Round Europe consists of six legs, ranging in length from 210-mile sprints to a 570-miler. With less than forty-eight hours between these, the race was as much a test for our shore crew as it was for the sailors. While the yacht was fighting the elements and the opposition, the shore team was battling their way around thousands of kilometres of European roads, often driving non-stop to beat the yacht into the next port.

In contrast to the French, the Spanish public was not particularly interested in the UAP race coming to town, and after two days of torrential rain, we were more than ready to leave again. The 450-mile leg to Cherbourg, a French Channel port, produced not only a tough race on the water, but had consequences in the protest room when Pierre Fehlman complained that we had failed to set a spinnaker pole in close proximity to our gennaker tack.

There proved to be some conflict between the IOR, which the boats are designed to, and the IYRU which established the main racing rules. Even the international jury was at odds over how to interpret the two rules and which took precedence. The protest dragged on late into the night as Grant and Pierre argued their cases. Fehlman was like a bear with a sore head. Not only had *New Zealand Endeavour* won the leg with ease, but *Merit Cup* had been beaten into third place by *La Poste*. After much

The three Farr maxi ketches bow to bow at the start of the Fastnet race.

heated debate, the Swiss skipper won his protest and we were penalised twelve minutes — not enough to deprive us of the leg win.

The irony of the whole debacle was that the day after the protest hearing, OMYA the governing body of the Whitbread maxis, convened to allow the practice of not having to fly a spinnaker pole when a gennaker was set. The protest brought home to us that we were back playing with the big boys again, and their favourite game was hardball. But this came as no big surprise. Our Whitbread campaigns have always attracted flak. In the previous race, it had been *Steinlager 2* and *Fisher and Paykel* that had been on the receiving end of cheating allegations from European rivals outsmarted by Kiwi ketch rigs.

Any complacency we may have felt had completely dissipated at the end of the next leg to Rotterdam, when once again we had dominated the race, only to find ourselves the victims of a confused race committee's bungled finishing procedure. Just as an athlete knows how to run straight and cross the finish line in a 100-metre sprint, professional yachtsmen know how to sail between two designated markers to complete a race. Approaching the illuminated finish line off the entrance to Europe's busiest seaport, we were concentrating hard in the dark to ensure we finished correctly. Race committee members were stationed not more than 50 metres away as *Endeavour* powered across the finish line, illuminated by a flashing buoy. Just as we started to

If you didn't have a job in the cockpit, you remained on the windward rail.

relax and began dropping our sails, we were astounded to hear a call on the radio telling us we had not finished the race correctly. Confusion reigned as we hurriedly rehoisted our sails, turned around and recrossed the finish in exactly the same direction we already had a few minutes earlier — this time to the satisfaction of the committee.

During the long motor up the river into Rotterdam, our blood was still boiling. We then faced another protest from *Merit Cup* over the incident, which they soon withdrew once the facts became clear. It seemed to us that the Europeans were hellbent on preventing us from winning their race. If they wanted war, so be it, but we had not come all this way to be penalised by a race official who could not see in the dark, or by our competitors bending rules to suit themselves.

ENZA, one of our seven sponsors, now enjoys a high profile in Europe, due in a large part to their sponsorship of yachts such as *New Zealand Endeavour* and Peter Blake's record-breaking *ENZA New Zealand*. To enhance the company's profile, Brian Aitken of ENZA had agreed to give us additional funding to enable us to compete in the Round Europe race. We were popular among the other competitors as we handed out ENZA apples, but when we gave the *Merit Cup* crew a boxful in Rotterdam, they were more than a little suspicious. It seemed they were familiar with the tale of Snow White and thought perhaps the apples were poisoned.

The Round Europe had never ventured into the Baltic Sea prior to this race, and the European media were making a big fuss about how difficult the Copenhagen–Helsinki–Stockholm legs would be. For us, the whole race was new territory, so the Baltic was only an extension of the unknown. One prominent French journalist was rendered speechless when, after asking Dalts what special preparation he had done for the Baltic legs, Grant replied 'Where's the Baltic?'

Our reason for doing the UAP race had been to size up our opposition and find our relative strengths and weaknesses. But if we had totally dominated the race, we would have been nervous. Human nature suggests that you always learn more from your mistakes or weaknesses than from your strengths. The two legs in the Baltic Sea were to highlight chinks in our armour.

Having led both legs for most of the way, we lost them in the closing stages in light winds. It might have been easy for us to say that we were just unlucky with the wind shifts, but we would have only been fooling ourselves. The fact was that we had a slight speed problem in light airs, particularly downwind. This was due to a combination of our sails being slightly off the pace and the boat being optimised a little too much for heavier winds. *Steinlager 2* had conclusively proved in the last Whitbread that in order to win you *must* be fast in light winds.

The final chapter of our Round Europe skirmish with *Merit Cup* occurred on the start line in Copenhagen. As we reached along the start line on starboard, which gave us the right of way, Pierre Fehlman came reaching in on port gybe and totally miscalculated his trajectory. As *New Zealand Endeavour* and the Swiss ketch closed range, Fehlman realised at the last minute that he had made an error in judgement. With nowhere to go, the two towering but fragile mizzen rigs collided at a combined speed of over 20 knots. The language directed from our deck to theirs was enough to make anyone wince. Fortunately, our mizzen spreaders were robust enough that our rig escaped intact. The same could not be said for *Merit Cup*, which was forced to return to the harbour to repair three broken spreaders. A red-faced Pierre Fehlman restarted the race three hours later with a bandaged rig to give chase to the fleet.

The finish of the final leg was at the entrance to the magnificent Stockholm Archipelago, which consists of literally thousands of islands. The three-hour motor into Stockholm gave us plenty of opportunity to reflect on the race. Apart from the obvious lessons learnt regarding *Endeavour*'s performance against the opposition, we had learnt a lot about how to sail the boat to its maximum potential. Probably the most valuable aspect of the race had been to transform the crew into a really tight and happy team. The rookie crew members had developed into immensely valuable players in the recently more relaxed environment on board, and Trev had done an outstanding job getting us around Europe, beating many of the top Euro' navigators in their own back yard.

In keeping with Kiwi yachting tradition, some serious partying took place upon our arrival in the centre of Stockholm. One of the highlights of the evening was the crew's impersonations of their skipper. Since time immemorial, Dalts has worn Ray Ban aviator sunglasses, the type made famous by Peter Fonda in the film *Easy Rider*. Most of the crew felt these would be more at home in MOTAT rather than on Dalts' head. The Ray Bans took a hammering at the party as everyone had a turn at being the skipper while pouring liquid attitude adjuster down their throats at great speed.

The arrival of Mike Quilter in Stockholm added to the enthusiasm within the team. Mike's immense talent and experience could only strengthen the crew, and for many of the guys it was something of a reunion. Having sailed as a watch captain on *Lion New Zealand* in the 1985 Whitbread, and as winning navigator on the all-conquering Big Red in the previous race, Lowlife had no trouble fitting in with his old crewmates. His easy-going nature and enthusiasm certainly helped to lighten the atmosphere on the boat whenever the going got tough.

With the Round Europe race successfully behind us, it was time to sail *New Zealand Endeavour* back to England. After a few days of sponsors commitments in London, she would be lifted out of the water to have a lighter keel fitted and, more importantly, have major surgery carried out on the bow. We had been fortunate not to encounter any really heavy weather during our extended tour of Europe, and George's temporary bow repair had done the job.

On the back of *Endeavour*'s success in the UAP race, things were heating up in the yachting media at home with Murray circulating his 'resignation' letter. Despite what was being said, *New Zealand Endeavour* had successfully and safely raced around Europe without any major problems in the electrical system.

Back at our base in Gosport, preparations were on schedule to replace the damaged bow sections and the keel. Tony Dalbeth and Paul Quinn from Marten Marine did most of the messy work, cutting out the damaged section of hull and replacing it with a newly fabricated section. Together with George, they achieved more in a week than the local builders would have in twice the time.

The new keel was some 500 kilograms lighter than the original and, being smaller, served to reduce public enemy number one in the boatspeed department — underwater drag. While the boat was undergoing surgery in the shed we took the opportunity to repaint the decks and recustomise the navigation station to Mike's specifications. The configuration of the offending batteries was changed to ensure the links could not work loose again.

Outside, Spike and Kev A battled the English weather, putting together our new mizzen and main masts. Although our existing rig was in excellent condition, Southern Spars had built a pair of new spars some 25 kilograms lighter. In stability terms, this was a considerable advantage and, coupled with new Kevlar rod rigging, made for a definite performance increase.

New Zealand Endeavour *crosses the finish line in Stockholm to take overall honours in the UAP Round Europe race.*

During the refit, Dalts, Shoebie and Foxy began seriously looking for a replacement for Colin Booth. With Mike Quilter recruited, the emphasis on finding the remaining new crew member had been put on the back burner. After considerable brainstorming, a short list of suitable candidates was compiled and we began to approach the various people. We looked first and foremost for a Kiwi sailor, although there were many highly experienced overseas yachties keen for a berth on *Endeavour*. By the end of the week, the name that stood out above the others was that of Stu Bannatyne. Hermie, as he was to be quickly nicknamed by the crew, had an impressive track record in the highly competitive Laser class. Originally from Wellington, Hermie had followed in the footsteps of Russell Coutts and John Irvine by winning the IYRU single-handed world youth championships. With an honours degree in mechanical engineering behind him, Hermie then focused his attention on the international match-racing circuit and was, conveniently, based in England. Although he had very little big-boat and offshore experience behind him, Hermie was very obviously a high-calibre helmsman, and you can never have too many of those on a Whitbread boat.

Throughout our stay in Gosport, we continued with our fitness programme. After considerable searching, Dalts and Trae found a local school gym with an instructor who was keen to help. On our first visit, we were all looking sideways at each other

A little over a week after winning the Round Europe, New Zealand Endeavour *sits in the boat shed undergoing major repairs.*

as Patrick Beresford had us doing jazzercise. Our misgivings proved to be short-lived, however, as he soon had us gasping for breath. We were to later find out that the super-enthusiastic Patrick was an ex-SAS fitness instructor.

With the boat rerated in its new configuration, we recommenced sail testing out in the English channel. Also undergoing trials were the pan-European entry *Intrum Justitia* and the Spanish boat *Galicia Pescanova*. During one particularly breezy day out in the Channel, Francisco Pino, one of the Spanish crewmen, had his hand torn off at the wrist in a freak accident. While he was coiling a halyard around a winch, the jammer failed and his hand was caught in a coil of rope under immense tension. A few weeks after the accident, Francisco was in good-enough humour to quip that he was now eligible to sail with the disabled and youth crew on *Dolphin and Youth*.

The dress rehearsal race before the start of the Whitbread was the prestigious Fastnet. To ensure that we learnt all we could, we had Bruce Farr and Russell Bowler on board to give us some objective feedback.

The race was to prove to be something of a benefit for the Whitbread 60s, with the fleet encountering fresh headwinds all the way to Fastnet Rock. As we bumped and crashed our way to windward, we watched enviously as the smaller boats, with the benefit of their water ballasting, blasted away to beat us to the Fastnet Rock by

The surgeons go to work removing the delaminated sections from the hull.

an hour and three-quarters. The maxis enjoyed a close tussle all the way to the rock, with *La Poste* leading us around by eight minutes. Those who had made the effort to watch the fleet round the famous lighthouse were treated to our spectacular lee-bow tack on *Merit Cup*, less than a boatlength off the surf-covered rocks, which gave us a five-second advantage as we set spinnakers for the slide back across the Irish Sea.

Any doubts we harboured about the change in configuration made to *New Zealand Endeavour* soon dissipated as we quickly stretched our lead on *Merit Cup* and inexorably ground *La Poste* down. By the time we had rounded the Scilly Isles for the final sprint back into Plymouth, we had a comfortable lead of five minutes over the French. The locals sitting on the hill-top lawn, made famous by Sir Francis Drake during the Armada invasion, witnessed a less hostile incursion into their harbour by a Spanish vessel, as *Galicia Pescanova* led the Fastnet fleet home by half an hour from *Winston* and *Intrum Justitia*. We led the maxis home, eight minutes ahead of *La Poste*, *Merit Cup* third.

Prior to the Fastnet, there had been much speculation about the potential performance of the newly revamped *Fortuna*, under the command of top English yachtsman Lawrie Smith. During the previous Whitbread, *Fortuna* had been a very fast heavy-airs downwind boat, but weak in other conditions. The Spanish tobacco giant Fortuna had spent considerable money converting her into a ketch and hiring Lawrie. It transpired that the major modifications had not had the desired effect, and *Fortune* was horribly off the pace during the Fastnet, finishing two and a half hours behind *Endeavour*.

A joke heard around Plymouth asked, 'What's the difference between Tin, Tin, Lassie and *Fortuna*?' The answer: 'Lassie and Tin Tin are movie stars, *Fortuna*'s just a dog!' Meanwhile, the British yachting press was quick to emphasise the maxis' comprehensive beating at the hands of the Whitbread 60s. One wit was overheard saying, 'Here come the dinosaurs', as the maxis entered the harbour. We were not overly concerned with the race result, as the conditions had strongly favoured the 60s and we had performed well against our maxi opposition.

Fortuna's poor performance saw Lawrie Smith go on the offensive, lashing out against the Farr maxis' bows. Smith claimed that they were nothing more than illegal carbon bowsprits. All of our expert advice indicated otherwise, and Bruce Farr had carefully researched the issue prior to the boats being built. Dalts believed the best form of defence was attack, and so he got stuck into *Fortuna*'s bumpkin. The radical fibreglass mizzen wing mast carried on *Fortuna* required additional support in the way of a bumpkin, which, by definition, is an outrigger. The backstays from the mizzen mast were lead through the bumpkin, as was the mizzen sheet. Dalts and Farr strongly believed that this practice of sheeting the mizzen through the bumpkin was illegal.

A bitter battle ensued in the British newspapers, as Smith launched personal attacks on Dalts and his sailing record. This tactic came as no great surprise, as four

years previously he had slagged Peter Blake. Lawrie appears to have a relatively limited repertoire of insults, judging from the way he raised the question, 'What's he [Dalton] ever won before?' Exactly the same comments he had made about Blakey. However, this sparring in the press was to hold little relevance in the near future, for Smith's Whitbread in the maxi class was to end when it had barely begun.

A welcome respite from Smith's media assault arrived in the *New Zealand Endeavour* office in Gosport a couple of weeks after the Fastnet, in the form of an anonymous fax. Some elementary investigative work revealed that the author of the following prose was Russell Bowler.

Pierre Fehlman was back for his fifth Whitbread with his new Merit Cup.

Hat Warning Prior to Whitbread '93

The crew of the Endeavour,
That mighty ketch-rigged boat,
Asked me to go racing
And supplied a hat and coat.

The start was quite a spectacle,
A Solent *full of sail.*
We set out for the rock
With Fortuna *on our tail.*

She did not stay there long,
She vanished in the fog.
Perhaps she needs tuning,
Or perhaps she's just a dog.

My watch began at midnight,
I went looking for my gear.
In the dark I could not find the stuff,
I was in complete despair.

Some prick had stole my coat and hat,
Essential when you're old.
Some prick was keeping nice and warm
While I was freezing cold.

In great distress I stole a hat,
I took it off the rack,
But the owner recognised it
And took the darn thing back.

It may amaze and shock you,
It caused me to be sick.
The exposure in windy weather
Due to some thoughtless prick.

I think the ship Endeavour
Will win the Whitbread race,
But watch out for the hat thief
Lurking around the place.

I won't say who I think it is,
It's not my place to squeal.
I hope he reads this plaintive tale
And feels a proper heel.

I won't tell on the bloody miser,
I won't let him deny the act
He stole my only headgear,
And that's a bloody fact.

I won't record his name in print
But I feel compelled to Grant
A warning to my crewmates,
His first name rhymes with aunt.

His second rhymes with Bolt On,
Which is what your hat should
be.
Use the wire to secure them
Before you go to sea.

Good fortune in the race,
Wear the bastards down.
I think you guys can do it,
Be first in every town.

In the week leading up to the start of the Whitbread race, there was a perceptible mood change within the *Endeavour* team. The long months of sometimes tedious preparation was about to come to an end and the fun stuff, the racing, was about to commence. The whole fleet was berthed in Southampton's Ocean Village for a week, enabling the public to get a closer look at what the Whitbread is all about. In contrast to previous starts, where the English had been indifferent, this race saw considerably greater interest.

We had gone to great lengths to ensure that the boat arrived in Southampton completely ready to race, with no last-minute work required to be done. *New Zealand Endeavour*, along with the other heavily Kiwi influenced campaigns, *Yamaha*, *Tokio* and *Winston*, were oases of calm compared to some of the other boats, on which crews frantically rushed about completing panic jobs.

Lowlife was keeping a very close eye on the weather maps in the days leading up to the start to ensure that he was fully armed with a comprehensive understanding of what conditions would prevail. He briefed the three watch captains, Shoebie, Foxy and Dalts, so they had an intimate understanding of where he wanted to go at what time and why. Based on his experience navigating *Steinlager 2* in the previous race, Lowlife had some firm ideas on which route down the Atlantic he felt was going to be the optimum. For the watch captains, and Dalts in particular, Mike's positive approach to his job filtered through, making for a confident environment before we embarked upon what is often the nautical equivalent of Russian Roulette.

The revamped Fortuna — *the radical fibreglass wing mast and the bumpkin protruding from the stern of the boat are clearly evident. (Inset) Lawrie Smith, our nemesis of four years ago, back to haunt us.*

CHAPTER FIVE

'Racing This Time . . .'

'I had no idea it would be so hard to say goodbye to everyone at the dock,' reflected Moose after we had left Southampton. 'On the one hand, all you want to do is get on with the race, and on the other, you don't want to say goodbye. After all of the preparation focusing completely on the race, the emotions you experience on the dock as you are about to throw off the lines kind of sneak up and catch you completely unaware.'

The day of the start was one of mixed emotions for the crew. The overriding sensation was that of relief. We were all keen to put the hype and drama of the final week's build-up behind us and get on with the job, though for the fathers on board the boat — Dalts, Shoebie, Trae and Mike — it was a new and difficult experience saying goodbye to their young.

Many of us were in a reflective frame of mind as we walked down the dock at Ocean Village, but we were soon shaken out of our reverie as an enthusiastic crowd of Kiwi supporters greeted us. As we climbed on board the boat, they let out a welcoming roar, not unlike a scaled-down version of the reception the All Blacks receive when running onto Eden Park for a test match. No matter how much of a battle-hardened veteran you are, it always gives an adrenalin rush to receive the sort of encouragement our compatriots were intent on giving us. George, our trusty shore-crew boat builder, had arranged for the local Whitbread radio station to play the stylised national anthem that is heard on Television New Zealand, to be broadcast. Our supporters were whipped into a frenzy of flag waving as we motored out of the harbour accompanied by 'God Defend New Zealand'. With our huge flag flying off the mizzen rig, few of our competitors would have underestimated the degree of national pride and support surrounding *New Zealand Endeavour.*

We were distracted from our thoughts when the cellphone we were carrying on board for television purposes rang. In theory, few people knew the number, but somehow Dalts' former *Fisher and Paykel* crew members had obtained it and called him up from Auckland.

The degree of professionalism and motivation among the crew was such that there was no need for Dalts to give any sort of a pep talk as we headed out to the start. Everyone knew what was required of him, and the conversation focused around the matter at hand: getting a good start and making our way into the English Channel without mishap.

With Dalts driving, Foxy calling tactics and Burt on the bow, we'd had plenty of practice at getting off the start line in good shape. The potential for damage to the boats while starting is high, as was graphically illustrated by the tangle suffered by *The Card* during the Auckland restart in the previous Whitbread. With this in mind,

Night approaches as we settle into the watch system that will rule our lives for the next three weeks.

the Whitbread race committee, with the help of the Coast Guard and the Navy, did an excellent job of clearing and maintaining a clear-water corridor for the fleet to sail through to clear the Solent.

As the resonant boom of the starting cannon faded away, it was Chris Dickson, in his first Whitbread, who threw down the gauntlet as he helmed *Tokio* out of the Solent in first place. Leaving the corridor, we had worked our way into second place, with *Winston* on our stern. We had some of the English television commentators confused when we set our mizzen gennaker and its bright-orange nylon sock remained stuck at the masthead instead of falling into the water for retrieval.

Leaving the Isle of Wight proved to be a bigger challenge than we had anticipated. *La Poste* had stolen a small lead on us as we reached out along the island coastline, after we had left our final gybe to the last Solent fairway mark too late. We soon became aware that Daniel Mallé's supporters were becoming a little too engrossed in our battle. To accommodate a legion of fans who had made the trip across the Channel to watch the start, the French postal service had chartered two cross-Channel ferries. One of these decided to join in on the fun and came within a couple of boatlengths of us as we duelled with *La Poste*. To avoid an imminent collision with the towering steel topsides of the ferry, we called for sea room on *La Poste*, who were obliged to give it to us. The result was that we were able to roll over the top of *La Poste*, stealing their wind and overtaking them in the process.

The same ferry was to provide even more spectacular entertainment soon afterwards, when it collided at full speed with the other one, the outcome being a gaping hole in the topsides of one of the ferries. From 200 metres away, the resounding crash as the two packed ferries collided was impressive, although it was a sobering thought to consider how serious the altercation could have been.

As we headed out into the English Channel, the Whitbread 60s were making it abundantly clear that they were going to be more than a little difficult than *La Poste* to shake off. Late afternoon saw the much-vaunted *Winston*, with Dennis Conner at the helm, sliding up from leeward and firmly attaching itself to our quarter-wave to 'catch a tow'. Dennis was providing us with a graphic demonstration of the skill that has won him four America's Cups as he kept *Winston*'s bow firmly locked to within a few feet of our stern for the best part of an hour. As Conner concentrated on staying locked onto our quarter-wave, his Kiwi co-skipper, Brad Butterworth, casually strolled onto the foredeck to offer us a packet of Winston cigarettes. Being sponsored by Smokefree, we graciously declined.

Our first night at sea quickly developed into a sail-changing frenzy, as the breeze constantly varied in both direction and strength — conditions that were to become the trademark of the leg. With *Endeavour*'s two masts and ability to carry up to five sails at once, a headsail or spinnaker change often produces a flow-on effect to the mizzen rig, and the combination there will also need attention. This insatiable appetite necessitated a sail change at every fifteen or twenty degrees of wind shift, and we soon worked our way through the complex inventory of 25 sails. Midway through the leg, after one particularly busy watch, Spike wrote in the log, 'Dalts promises us a stress-free standby watch — we wait!'

The first major headache to confront our trusty navigator was the infamous Ushant Channel, which separates the English Channel from the Bay of Biscay. With tides of up to six knots ripping around this treacherous coastline off the north-western tip of France, an incorrect decision by Mike could have been a significant disadvantage. However, our experience of this coastline a few months earlier gave us confidence and we shot through the tidal gate like an orange pip and out into a fresh north-westerly wind that we would ride for the next few days.

The fleet's pecking order soon established itself as we began to settle into the watch routine that would rule our lives for the next three weeks. While we were narrowly leading the maxis from a much-improved *Fortuna*, *Tokio* had capitalised on its strong start in the Solent to claim a lead over Ross Field's *Yamaha*, a short distance in front of us.

When the wind strength increased, Shoebie noticed that the mizzen rig was starting to behave in a disturbing manner. 'Get this mizzen gennaker off now!' was his rapid command as the rig began inverting between the deck and the first spreaders. This phenomenon occurred when the mizzen boom vang pushed the bottom panel

Mike plots the fleet's positions onto the chart.

of the mast sideways. The result of this could very easily have been disastrous as the boat crashed and banged its way through the large bumpy seaway.

Once we had the wobbly mizzen mast back under control with a smaller staysail set, we observed how well Lawrie Smith's *Fortuna* was performing after an unspectacular debut in the Fastnet race. While we were having to reduce sail area to keep the mizzen in one piece, *Fortuna* was still flying her full-sized mizzen gennaker off the radical fibreglass wing mast. Suddenly, as we sat in the cockpit watching *Fortuna*, we witnessed her massive mizzen mast crash into the sea. We could not help but feel some empathy for Smith and his crew — you do not wish that sort of bad luck on anyone. As *Fortuna*'s crew began their depressing clean-up operation, she rapidly disappeared over the horizon behind us.

We later found out that the dismasting was caused by the failure of the controversial bumpkin supporting the top mast backstays, which hold the mizzen mast up when running downwind with a gennaker set. Smith decided to withdraw from the race after talking with his Spanish sponsors, then suffered further embarrassment when, on the sail back to the south coast of England, *Fortuna* broke her main mast too.

Although one of our major competitors had gone, which would obviously improve our prospects of winning, the maxi fleet had diminished in stature both in numbers and profile with the demise of *Fortuna*. The battle between the maxis and the Whitbread 60s for media attention was to become hard-fought throughout the rest of the race, with some of the smaller-boat skippers frequently making reference to the diminished size of the maxi fleet.

Meanwhile, we were encouraged on board *Endeavour* to discover that in the hard running conditions we were encountering across the Bay of Biscay that not only were we putting time on our maxi rivals, but we were also able to hang on reasonably well with the leading 60s, with our ability to carry mizzen gennakers in up to 40 knots of wind.

As the fleet blasted past Cape Finisterre off the north-west corner of Spain and headed out into the Atlantic Ocean for the dash south towards the Equator, those of us who had participated in the previous Whitbread recalled that it was at this stage that *Steinlager 2* had sprinted to an unassailable lead. Mike Quilter had sat in *Steinlager*'s navigation station sweating over decisions that could make or break the race and he was experiencing a sense of *déjà vu* on *Endeavour*.

The role of navigator has dramatically changed in the past decade. Their primary job used to be to plot the position of the boat and try to assimilate any weather data he could from radio to complement 'head out the window' forecasting. Today's racing navigator is more of a computer boffin, capable of analysing information from electronic equipment that would not be out of place in the cockpit of a jumbo jet. In the place of the traditional sextant is the GPS (Global Positioning System), now found

This weatherfax map indicates an intense low-pressure system centred over France. (below) This 'Feedback' weather satellite photo was received on board at the same time as the weatherfax and shows the same low-pressure system. The arrow indicates New Zealand Endeavour*'s position.*

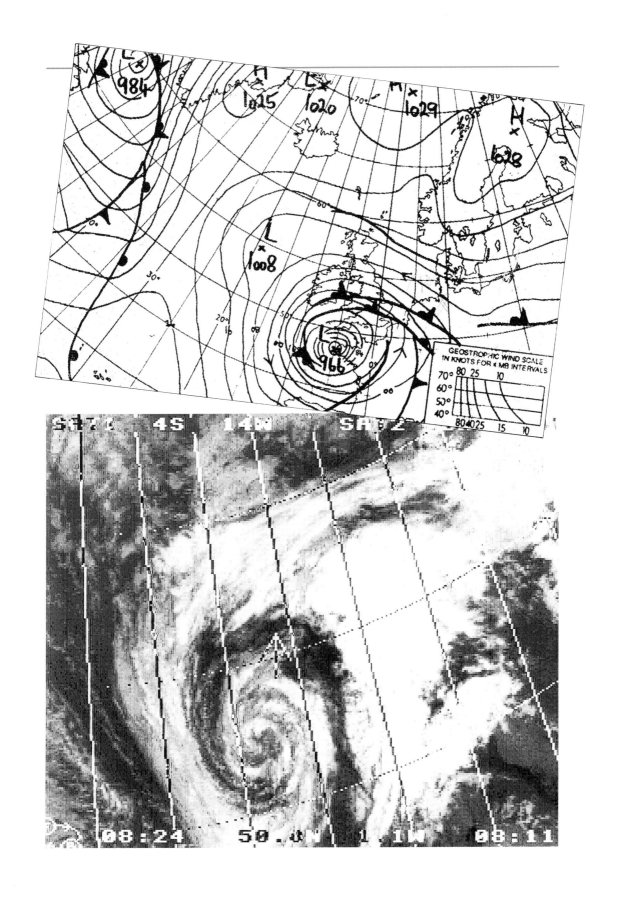

on almost every offshore yacht. By Mike's own tongue-in-cheek admission, he is not even sure how to open the sextant case.

Because he can rely on the GPS to tell him where the boat is, Mike's primary concern is to analyse data from the weatherfax, which can be programmed to receive maps from stations around the world. These are transmitted by short-wave radio signal, the only drawback being that atmospherics of the sky can occasionally hinder reception. The map is digitised into a computer where a software package known as MacSea can suggest an optimum course through the prevailing weather system.

This might sound as though the navigator has all of his work done for him, but Mike only uses the computer as a self-check against his gut feeling and experience in analysing the maps himself. There are two other systems for gathering weather data. A satellite receiver that captures photographic images is useful for picking up frontal activity, particularly in the Southern Ocean where there are limited weather fax maps available. Another system, called Neptune, commonly referred to as the 'Grib file' came from the French meteorological bureau, Meteo France, via British Telecom and Inmarrsat. The data arrived in telex form through the Satcom C and was converted into the Macintosh system being used on most of the boats. With five days of information available, this system was probably the most valuable weather analysis tool that we had on board.

On-board computer systems are also used to run tests — recording and logging all the information the sailing instruments generate and then examining the difference between different sail combinations. While we could incessantly argue amongst ourselves for hours on deck as to what combination was fastest, by running a test on the computer we could come up with a definitive result.

As well as his navigational duties, Mike ran the inter-yacht position sched when it was *Endeavour*'s turn and plotted our competitors when their positions came in. But it was probably his self-appointed role as chocolate policeman that Mike took the most seriously. A self-confessed chocoholic, he would whip himself into a frenzy if supplies were running short towards the end of a leg and used to take it upon himself to stash the remaining bars in the navigation station. From this position of power, Mike assumed the role of a mafia Don, issuing chocolate to the rest of the crew in return for a tax — a large chunk of the bar.

In contrast to four years ago, there were no big breaks to be had this time on the first leg and the fleet remained reasonably tightly bunched as we headed south towards blue seas and sunshine. The hallmark of this leg has been fresh north-easterly trade winds from off the coast of Spain all the way south towards the Equator. We decided that whoever organised the weather for us must have forgotten this tradition, as we encountered much lighter than usual trades. However, these were very much to *New Zealand Endeavour*'s liking, and we enjoyed a speed edge over the rest of the fleet on the procession south.

If the wind strength was a little lower than normal, the temperature certainly

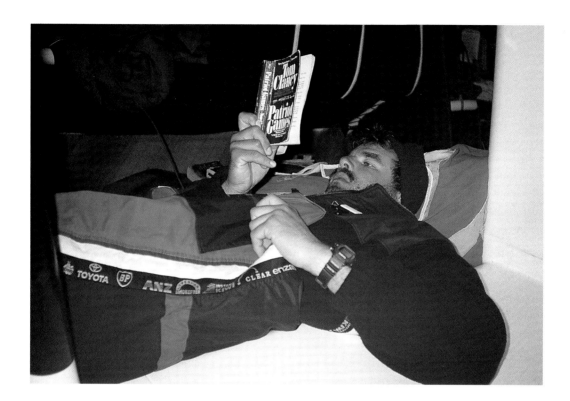

was not. After the cool English weather we had become accustomed to, the intense heat of the tropics came as a bit of a shock and fans were soon working overtime as the interior of the boat took on the ambience of a sauna. The off-watch crew lay in their bunks gasping like stranded goldfish. The most popular pastime was listening to the communal Walkmans and reading, as sleep became almost impossible in the intense heat. On deck, however, we worked overtime trying to work our way through a series of calms. Progress became a little like a game of snakes and ladders: two steps forward and one back. We were starting to wonder that if this is what the trade winds are like, what is going to happen in the doldrums?

The variable weather conditions resulted in frequent spinnaker and gennaker peels to keep the boat sailing at its optimum. *Endeavour*'s masts were fitted with halyard locks to keep the weight down at the top of the rigs, but this meant that the bowmen had to be hoisted aloft in Larakis harnesses to clip the spinnaker halyards off onto a strop. Each of the three bowmen customised his harnesses, often incorporating a few basic accessories like tape, a knife and small spanner to carry out any repairs while up the mast. Burt was forever getting a hard time from the rest of the crew about the way he always managed to stay impeccably groomed, even in the most adverse conditions, and an anonymous comedian suggested in the log that

Reading books was the most popular off-watch pastime.

it was time to run a 'Design Burt a Larakis Competition'. The list eventually included: a rechargeable hair dryer, hairbrush and comb, Fabergé body deodorant, a spare pair of silk boxer shorts, nail file and clippers, and a hand-held mirror.

As we settled into our routine of four-hourly watches, a few intriguing character traits began to emerge among the crew. Hermie was finding the Whitbread very different from the cut and thrust world of Laser racing. It was not long before he was the brunt of some sharp humour for his incredible conservation of energy on deck. When asked why he was so slow, he casually replied, 'Speed when required!' This prompted us to give him the alternative nickname Flash. One note in the logbook claimed that 'Hermie has vowed not to sleep as much. With only a few days to go, I wouldn't say he was pushing the envelope.' Offsetting this inactivity, was Hermie's incredible capacity for devouring vast quantities of food at an amazing rate.

Skunk had made a £10 bet with his watch captain, Shoebie, that he would be able to make it through the first week at sea 'without stinking'. Despite protestations that it wasn't him, some particularly undesirable fumes emanating from Skunk's general vicinity on deck during a night watch was all it took for him to lose the bet.

As the fleet progressed down the Atlantic, we heard through news reports that *La Poste* had badly twisted her mizzen mast and could only set sail on it in the lightest of airs. This effectively eliminated any chances of overall victory for the French, and our only serious threat in the maxi class was *Merit Cup*.

The six-hourly satellite position reports were eagerly awaited. In previous races, the only chance we had to find out how we were going against our opposition were twelve-hourly inter-yacht radio scheds. The advent of satellite scheds meant that we could keep much closer tabs on what the other yachts were up to. On the one hand, it reduced the risk of one of our competitors making a break we did not know about, but on the other, it made it harder for us to make a jump by sailing a different course. The big break that *Steinlager 2* made during the first leg of the previous race would have been significantly harder to pull off under the Satcom position-reporting system. Waiting for the positions to be received on board was not unlike anticipating exam results. It was definitive proof as to whether we were sailing the boat well and were positioned in the best weather conditions. A good sched would see smiles all around and the results would quickly be relayed to the on-watch crew, a bad sched would be met with grim faces down below and often not find its way to the guys on deck.

As well as providing us with fleet position reports, the Satcom system enabled us to communicate by fax with the outside world. Thus Shoebie got a message that his eighteen-month-old son Thomas was ill and had been admitted to hospital for four days. While it is great to be able to communicate with home, there are times when news from the outside can make life on board worrying and frustrating.

On day thirteen we arrived in the doldrums, the notorious band of calms just north of the Equator, separating the north-easterly trades from the south-easterlies. For centuries this area of the ocean has been a source of frustration for seafarers. It

was not uncommon for a sailing ship to be held captive for weeks in a vice-like grip. For the modern ocean racing yachtsmen, the doldrums can be equally as infuriating.

The doldrum's notorious calms are occasionally disturbed by short and vicious squalls generated by towering black cumulo-nimbus clouds. It is these that normally spirit a yacht out into the south-east trades. Unfortunately for us, these squalls were missing this time and we were confronted with calms and more calms.

Having worked our way into a 48-mile lead over *Merit Cup*, we were very unimpressed to see her sail up over the horizon and draw level with us to the west. In the previous 24 hours we had made a painfully slow 108 miles, the nautical equivalent of a snail's pace and the slowest run any of us could remember in our Whitbread race experience.

Floating in the windless void was, if nothing else, a great lesson in humility. An eternal optimist would call it character building, but to us it was just plain frustrating to see two weeks' work evaporate.

The general mood was summed up by the following logbook entry: 'My father always told me, "Son don't let yachting become your job; keep it as a sport, a hobby, something you can look forward to on the weekends and above all, make it fun".' In our current frame of mind, most of us found ourselves wishing we had listened to that gem of paternal advice.

The most commonly used sails for the three days we remained ensnared in the

Trae looks in vain for wind as we sit completely becalmed in the doldrums. (next page) The windseeker hangs motionless above a glassy sea.

doldrums were the light genoa and a gossamer-thin windseeker, which caught every little zephyr of breeze. As the wind speed built, we would rehoist the light genoa, and then peel straight back to the windseeker as soon as it faded. It was during one of these peels between sails under cover of darkness that a wayward flying fish misjudged its trajectory and landed in the folds of the windseeker as it was being packed. The stench that began to emanate from within the boat soon became unbearable in the intense heat, and we indulged in much finger pointing. Initially, Burt's boots were considered the culprit, and it was not until a couple of days later, when we pulled the windseeker back on deck to rehoist it, that we discovered the badly decomposed fish in the folds of the sail.

By the time we wriggled free of the doldrums, we had re-established much of our previous lead over *Merit Cup*. Chris Dickson and his multi-national team on board *Tokio* were continuing to assert their dominance over the rest of the Whitbread 60s and were less than twenty miles astern of us as we began our sprint towards the South American coast.

Tucked away in an 85-foot black-lined cocoon, life can become pretty boring and it was necessary to generate our own entertainment and humour. It was not surprising, then, that the traditional Equator-crossing ceremony was cranked up into a major event on the *Endeavour* social calendar. A testament to the level of experience

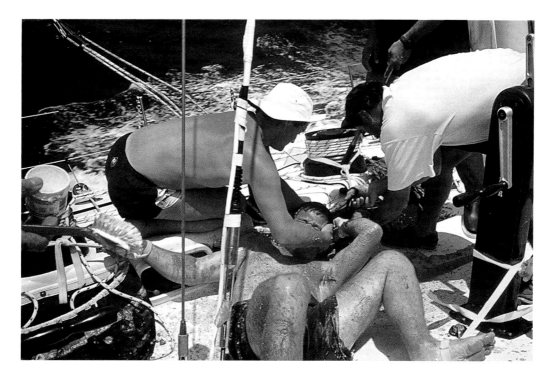

BC and Lowlife's sadistic streaks emerged as they doused Moose in swill and altered his hairstyle.

among the crew was the fact that only two of the guys, Moose and Hermie, had not previously sailed across 'the line'.

Hidden sadistic streaks often come to the fore at this time and the normally laid-back characters like BC and Lowlife undergo extreme personality changes. BC used his experience from his two previous Whitbreads to create the swill that Moose and Hermie would be forced to swallow. This consisted of all of the left-over freeze-dried food scraps from the last few days, combined with a dose of yeast to ensure it was 'just right'. BC was so impressed with his creation that he immediately named it Chateau Swill '93, Private Bin — its bouquet was not dissimilar to that of the rotting flying fish. Once the line-crossing ceremony was complete and the newly indoctrinated members of King Neptune's realm were untied after losing the obligatory chunk of hair and appearing before the kangaroo court, it took half an hour to wash the residue swill out through the cockpit drains. Throughout the ceremony the boat continued to be raced at full potential, with the helmsman and trimmers watching events in the cockpit with a detached amusement.

In addition to the ever-present flying fish, there was an abundance of sea life as we sailed south, ranging from turtles to sharks and dolphins. It is the dolphins that are always the most spectacular as they perform acrobatics alongside the boat. They are even more impressive at night, carving trails of luminescence through the black sea and giving the appearance of torpedoes racing towards a target.

Brad and Trae convert BC's galley into a sail loft to repair a torn spinnaker.

While *New Zealand Endeavour* continued to lead the fleet from *Tokio* and *Merit Cup*, there was a constantly changing pattern further astern. The doldrums and lighter-than-usual trade winds had toyed with the bulk of the fleet, with fortunes being made and lost on a daily basis.

Once back into the Southern Hemisphere and into the steadier trades, we made good pace down the Brazilian coast towards Rio de Janeiro. The further south we sailed, the further aft the breeze shifted, enabling us to set our big spinnakers and mizzen gennakers. Life was pretty pleasant as we slid through the aqua-coloured seas and cloudless skies. On deck, even in the middle of the night, the only clothes required were a pair of shorts and a T-shirt. To make our life even more enjoyable, the regular position reports showed us inexorably creeping away from *Tokio* and *Merit Cup*. Back in the bunch, *Yamaha* was having a surprisingly tough time. With the amount of preparation her team had put in, we had expected to see them right at the head of the fleet.

A bowman spends much of his working day up the mast. Sean is being hoisted up the mast to clear the halyards.

The winds increased until we were sailing at 'full noise' — maximum spinnakers and mizzen gennakers set in conditions that kept us on our toes. It was in this hard downwind running at the same stage of the previous race that *Fisher and Paykel* had broken its mizzen mast and Dalts became distinctly edgy as *Endeavour* blasted at breakneck speeds. It was not until we were well clear of *Fisher and Paykel*'s 'drop zone' that he began to relax again. The guys who had sailed on board *Steinlager 2* could not see what all the fuss was about, but by the time we were to arrive in Fremantle at the completion of leg two, everyone knew exactly what must have been going through Dalts' mind off the Brazilian coast.

As we approached Uruguay, the consistent northerly wind flow gave way to a more unstable weather pattern. One evening a visit from the infamous pampero provided us with a graphic demonstration of the forces of nature. Midway through the meal and twenty minutes before watch change, *Endeavour* was surfing down waves under full spinnaker and mizzen gennaker as dusk rapidly consumed the clear sky. In a period of a few short minutes, a 'roll cloud', the calling card of a pampero, formed on the southern horizon. As Foxy instructed his watch to prepare to drop the spinnaker and gennaker if necessary, the cloud began to increase both in size and intensity at an alarming rate. A hurried call to get the standby watch on deck ready for some action came barely in time, as the cloud approached us with the speed and intensity of a runaway freight train.

No sooner was the standby watch on deck, than we were thumped by a 35-knot squall and driving rain from completely the opposite direction. The spinnaker

Quick hands are needed to haul the mizzen gennaker back on deck.

and gennaker were hurriedly dropped and the boat shook violently as the Kevlar mainsail and mizzen thrashed angrily. By virtue of some sharp crew work, we were able to get the boat back up to pace and on course within a few minutes. Foxy commented wryly, 'You wouldn't want to be hit by that bastard at night-time,' which is exactly what happened to the boats astern of us a few hours later as the pampero smashed its way through the fleet.

Within hours of this furious blow passing over us, the wind swung back into the north, enabling us to reset our downwind sails for the remaining uneventful miles into Punta del Este. *New Zealand Endeavour* would have made a spectacular sight, surfing at speeds in excess of twenty knots, had there been any boats out on the water to witness our arrival at Punta.

Dalts found it impossible to conceal the huge grin on his face as he helmed *Endeavour* across the finish line to win his first Whitbread leg as a skipper. After playing second fiddle to Peter Blake and *Steinlager 2*, he had finally stepped into the spotlight. His elated crew lowered the sails for the motor into the arrival pontoon for an urgent appointment with several cold Heinekens.

The psychological advantage of winning the first leg in the Whitbread has historically proved to be invaluable. With the winning margin in excess of eight hours over *Merit Cup*, the result was all we could have hoped for. An old adage says that 'winners are grinners', and the smiles on our faces that first night in Punta del Este were broad indeed.

Scorching past Fisher and Paykel's 'drop zone'.

Leg One: Southhampton — Punta del Este (6281 miles)

Class	Boat Name	Days	Hours	Minutes	Secs	Overall Position After Leg	Average Speed for Leg
Maxi	New Zealand Endeavour	24	07	19	02	1	10.8
W 60	Tokio	24	10	28	21	2	10.7
Maxi	Merit Cup	24	15	41	39	3	10.6
W 60	Galicia 93 Pescanova	24	20	30	42	4	10.5
W 60	Yamaha	24	21	30	22	5	10.5
W 60	Winston	24	23	49	45	6	10.4
W 60	Intrum Justitia	25	02	40	49	7	10.4
Maxi	La Poste	25	18	03	28	8	10.2
W 60	Dolphin and Youth	26	03	22	02	9	10.0
W 60	Brooksfield	26	03	35	09	10	10.0
W 60	US Women's Challenge	27	19	23	45	11	9.4
Maxi	Uruguay Natural	28	04	43	37	12	9.3
W 60	Hetman Sahaidachny	28	06	32	57	13	9.3
W 60	Odessa	40	22	31	39	14	6.4

CHAPTER SIX

Fremantle or Bust

Being first into Punta del Este meant more than just winning the opening and, in many ways, trickiest leg of the Whitbread. It served to solidify our team, and was also the acid test as to whether the three years of planning and preparation that had gone into *New Zealand Endeavour* were on track. In our first major opportunity to go head to head with the competition, we had prevailed against our maxi rivals and the Whitbread 60s. So far, things were looking good.

With the exception of *La Poste*'s damaged mizzen mast, the fleet arrived in Punta in good shape, with minimal work required to prepare them for the next leg into the infamous Southern Ocean. Our four weeks in Punta saw us stripping down all the winches and deck hardware for servicing and going over rigs and sails with a fine-tooth comb. But even though our maintenance schedule was extensive, it did not take long for us to start running out of jobs.

One of the drawbacks of Punta was that, although it is South America's most popular holiday destination, there is little to do there for entertainment out of season. As was the case in the last race, many of the sailors headed out to one of Punta's magnificent golf courses. Heineken did a great job of organising a tournament among the crews that was such a success it was repeated in each subsequent stopover. There were a few hot-shot golfers in the fleet including our own Spike and Brad, who became the team to beat at each tournament. Ever the perfect hosts, Vicki Stacey and her Heineken team placed coolers of their product at each tee. In the heat, this was quickly consumed and had some amusing effects. As the round progressed, an increasing number of drives were hooked and sliced, and wayward balls abandoned in the rough.

The first of many crew changes that were to take place throughout the Whitbread occurred in Punta. *Intrum Justitia*'s Swedish skipper Roger Nilson was replaced by our old nemesis Lawrie Smith. There had been murmurs of dissatisfaction among the crew of *Intrum* after mediocre performances in the Round Europe and Fastnet races, but it was a surprise when the boat's management negotiated a contract with Smith, freshly back in England with his mastless *Fortuna*. Nilson, it was announced, had 'resigned' as a result of a continuing knee problem that required surgery. It must have been a bitter blow for the Swede, who had set up the project in the first place. He need not have felt lonely, as he was to be joined on the sidelines by several other high-profile competitors as the race progressed. Considering the fact that the *Fortuna* campaign had ended in such an embarrassing disaster, we were amazed that the British yachting media were quite so tame when Smith arrived in Punta to take over *Intrum Justitia*.

The next casualty on this front was Nance Frank, skipper of the *US Women's Challenge*. Her crew had arrived in Punta a dispirited bunch after a lacklustre

Burt begins the depressing job of cutting down the broken section of mizzen mast.

performance on the leg from Southampton. The yacht club in Punta became a place of huddled conversations and clandestine meetings as some of Frank's senior crew members sought to oust her from her own campaign. Remarkably, they succeeded.

After much manoeuvring, Frank withdrew from the race, citing insufficient funds. With less than a week remaining to the start of the second leg, the boat's owners, Ocean Ventures, re-entered the newly named *Women's Challenge* and appointed the highly experienced Dawn Riley as skipper. If things had been a little dull in Punta early on, things soon hotted up with constant speculation as to what was going to happen next.

The last few days turned out to be relatively peaceful — except for the weather. A storm lashed the Punta del Este peninsula, making it impossible to walk down the breakwater to the yachts. Those that did attempt this played a game of chicken with the thundering surf. After several people had been picked up and washed into the sea, the Uruguayan Navy placed a guard to prevent anyone getting down to the boats. We had a nervous time watching the yachts being buffeted by breaking surf and storm-force winds. In the back of our minds, we also knew the storm was giving us an insight into what lay ahead on our imminent plunge into the Southern Ocean.

Many of the British yachting journalists in Punta were writing off the prospects of *New Zealand Endeavour* winning the second leg. Although we knew the Whitbread

Brad displays the style that took he and Spike to the top of the leader board in the Heineken golf tournament.

60s were going to be a major handful, we were quietly optimistic that, with a bit of luck, we could upset the predictions and be first into Fremantle. In any case, we were more than happy to go into this leg as the underdog.

The morning of the start dawned wet and cold, with a blustery south-easterly wind whipping across the harbour. Breakfast that morning was a very quiet affair, with everyone nervously looking out the window and aware that we would face head winds and big seas for at least the first day. Several hours later, as we hoisted our sails in the strong winds, there was a mood of resolute determination among the crew. For the six rookies on board *Endeavour*, it was time to see if all of the stories they had heard about the Southern Ocean were true. We all felt a mix of trepidation and excitement as we set out to race into the most challenging seas in the world, where even the slightest sign of disrespect to the elements is dealt with harshly.

One of the crew of the local entry *Uruguay Natural* evidently had second thoughts about whether this leg was really for him. As the boat sailed around the start line, he leapt over the side and swam across to one of the nearby spectator boats. His puzzled crewmates were left to concentrate on getting on with the race one crew member short. A couple of weeks later, battling our way through the frozen wastes of the Southern Ocean, there were a few private thoughts as to whether or not the Uruguayan crewman had been so crazy after all.

The storm that lashed Punta del Este gave us an insight into what lay ahead in the Southern Ocean.

Intrum Justitia immediately showed the benefit of a change in skipper by leading the fleet away from Punta, with *Endeavour* hard on her heels. As we turned to head upwind on the long trek south, life became very bumpy. With the wind increasing to 35 knots, a change from the number 3 to the number 5 jib was required to depower the boat. It is in these conditions that the bowmen really earn their keep, fighting to keep control of sails on the foredeck while the boat does its best to toss them overboard. During this sail change, Burt and Sean completely disappeared underwater a couple of times when the boat pitched into breaking seas. Our first gear damage occurred in the form of a broken stanchion when the jib was dragged aft to be packed on the windward rail.

The Whitbread 60s were soon giving a graphic demonstration of their awesome upwind power, as they charged into the seaway with their water ballast tanks filled up. It was only a couple of good windshifts called by Mike in the middle of the night that kept us on the front row of the grid. Things can become very confusing at night trying to keep track of the opposition on the radar and keeping an eye on their navigation lights. It requires a special aptitude not to become disorientated and miss a critical windshift, and so find yourself a couple of miles behind.

During our first night at sea, the on-watch crew members were drinking coffee to keep themselves awake. Midway gulping his down, Foxy discovered white lumps floating in his cup. Close inspection with a torch revealed that the coffee had been mixed with flour rather than milk powder. It was obvious we had a phantom on board, as no one would own up to mixing flour and water in the milk container. It was widely agreed that this style of coffee would never become popular in the trendy cafés.

The rough and tumble soon gave way to light to moderate breezes, which prevailed for the next two days as the fleet headed southwards at a relatively sedate pace. The maxis revelled in the conditions and we found ourselves at the head of the position scheds, just in front of *Merit Cup*.

On day three we were soon shaken out of our trance when a dramatic increase in both wind strength and sea size, and an equally dramatic decrease in temperature, heralded our arrival into the Southern Ocean.

The next day a sequence of events occurred that prompted us to call this Spike's Big Day. As the dull dawn light began to break up the dark sky, an increase in wind strength necessitated a spinnaker peel. Spike, as the on-watch bowman, climbed out to the end of the spinnaker pole to clip the tack of the new sail onto the pole. While he was hanging onto the outboard end of the pole some six metres above the roaring bow wave, the topping lift supporting the outboard end of the pole was inadvertently released. The first that Spike knew of the problem was when he found himself suddenly plunged into seven-degree water. Still clipped onto the end of the pole, he was being dragged at speeds in excess of seventeen knots. With the spinnaker pole pinned against the sidestays, and Spike spending more time below the water than above it, there

Spike goes through his aerial acrobatic routine as he attempts to put a chafe patch on the mainsail.

was frantic activity around the mast as crewmen struggled to bounce the topping lift up and pull him clear of the frigid water. After what seemed like an eternity, the spinnaker pole and the bedraggled bowman were eventually hoisted clear of the water. If ever we needed any reminding that prudence and care were needed in this part of the world, it was reinforced by this incident.

To cap off Spike's day, he was called upon to retrieve the spinnaker, which was jammed at the top of the rig in 40 knots of wind. After his experience earlier in the morning, it was amazing that we managed to get him off the deck at all, but Spike is one of that rare breed — a bowman — who thrives 30 metres up a violently moving mast.

No sooner had Spike returned to the deck, having successfully retrieved the jammed spinnaker, than he took the helm. Within a matter of minutes, he launched the boat down an enormous wave, recording a new speed record of 28.4 knots.

As the fleet headed on the great circle course towards Fremantle, the temperature continued to drop at an inversely proportional rate to the increasing latitude and the days became longer, until we had no more than six hours of darkness. The sun, however, was mostly absent, but on one of the rare occasions it made a guest appearance, Hermie donned sunglasses at four thirty in the morning while trimming the spinnaker. Some of us were not convinced that he was not just trying to look cool.

A pitch-black night can turn a relatively easy daytime deck job into a major mission. In order to preserve the helmsman's all-important vision, torches are kept to a minimum, so tasks tend to take a lot longer to perform and there is an increased margin for error. Shortly after midnight on our fourth night at sea, one such mishap occurred when Dalts' watch gybed the boat in 25 knots of wind. With Shoebie's standby watch up on deck to help out, everything was set for the manoeuvre. As Dalts called 'Gybing' and began to turn the boat through its arc onto the new starboard gybe, things began to go wrong in the back of the boat.

Unfortunately, the mizzen sheet had overridden when it was loaded onto the self-tailer, the device on top of the winch that enables the sheet to pull itself in as the winch turns. Such an override is one of the yachtsman's biggest enemies, as it winds the heavily laden sheet into an impossible tangle. Calls of 'Ease the sheet!' from Dalts, as the mizzen filled with wind on the new gybe and began to screw the boat into a broach, were returned with an anxious response of 'I can't!' from Shoebie who was frantically trying to untangle the override. Dalts' plaintive yells to sort out the mess were drowned out by the noise of the angrily thrashing sail cloth.

BC, who had been on deck for the manoeuvre, thought that perhaps Dalts had just discovered that he still had the rental car keys in his pocket and had decided to return to Punta to give them back. Trae, an aspiring musician, decided to write a song about the broach. Sung to the tune of Englebert Humperdinck's 'Please Release Me', it went something like this:

Please release me, let me go,
For I am trying to steer one five oooooohhhh.
We gybed and the mizzen wasn't let go.
Please release me, come on, boys, let me go.
With the helm hard down, Daltsy's arms started to grow.
He screamed for f...'s sake give me some floooooohhhh.
All I wanted was to gybe and go.
So please release me, come on, boys, it's time to go.

The afternoon after our impromptu turn back towards Punta, the wind freshened and changed direction, giving us an extended period of 'blast' reaching. This term comes from the fact that reaching across the wind under jib top is both very fast and extremely wet. In these conditions we took on the appearance of drowned rats, as the boat surged down moving walls of the Southern Ocean at speeds well in excess of twenty knots. For the helmsman, it was a case of lining the boat up on the wave then dipping his head to avoid the spray lashing his face.

Hands became blocks of ice by the end of a four-hour watch on deck at high latitudes. Many of the younger guys had bought flash dry-suit diving gloves in England before the race. The 'vets' had told them these were not necessary, but we had obviously forgotten how cold it got down south. After one particularly cold watch, Foxy arranged to borrow Trae's bright-orange 'wonder gloves' for the agreed fee of

After a four-hour watch on deck, our bodies turned into iceblocks.

providing him with all the alcohol he could drink in one night once we had arrived in Fremantle. It is amazing what you will do to stay warm.

If standing a four-hour watch on deck in these conditions was akin to living on a half-tide rock in a storm, life down below decks was not a whole lot better. A combination of the ever-present condensation dripping off the deck head and the large volumes of water that pour down the hatch when a sail was being lowered down below resulted in the interior being perpetually soaked. On one occasion, Hermie drove the boat under spinnaker down one particularly steep wave and straight into the back of the next. The cockpit was filled to the brim with freezing water, a good percentage of which went down into the interior of the boat through the partially open hatch. He had obviously decided he was a U-boat commander but had forgotten to shut the hatches before diving.

At 50 degrees south, after three days of blast reaching, we enjoyed a welcome reprieve in the form of some clear skies and lighter winds. Mike was a little concerned that we would be caught out by a ridge of high pressure and hung out to dry, as we were one of the most northerly boats in the fleet. Memories of *Fisher and Paykel* scorching away to a big lead over *Steinlager 2* were hard for Mike to forget, and he was studying the weatherfax maps with increasing anxiety. As luck would have it, the ridge and its associated light winds trapped the boats further to the south. When things were going well for us, with our lead increasing at each six-hourly sched, Mike was the most popular guy on the boat. It is all very well to be sailing the boat hard and fast up on deck and driving it to its full potential, but if the navigator makes an

Merit Cup *also displayed U-boat tendencies.*

error of judgement in his analysis of the water, all the toil can be for nothing if the opposition is in better wind.

Despite the clearer skies and lighter breezes, the temperature still remained extremely cold. As dusk fell on our ninth day at sea, the temperature snapped to below freezing and the whole boat was soon covered in a coating of ice from the masthead to the deck. Even our masthead wand, which measures wind speed and direction, froze up and had to be retrieved and thawed out over the galley primus. In these conditions, moving around the boat became dangerous, with our thick rubber boots slipping and sliding all over the slick and lurching deck.

By now we were well and truly into iceberg territory, and a member of the standby watch was constantly sitting in the nav station keeping an eye on the radar for any bergs that may be in our path but invisible in the darkness. The big ones are relatively easy to pick up as ghostly green blips, but the smaller chunks of ice that have been broken off the main iceberg are a constant worry. These are known as growlers and can be as small as a car or as big as a house.

While they are potentially dangerous, icebergs are one of the features that make the Southern Ocean a wonderfully spectacular place. The sight of huge seas crashing against the vertical cliff faces of these bergs, enormous albatrosses with three-metre wing spans skimming the wave tops behind the boat, and the half-terrifying, half-exhilarating sailing makes this part of the globe irresistible.

New Zealand Endeavour proved to be considerably faster in the heavy running and reaching conditions that are so prevalent in the Southern Ocean than her

Icebergs were our constant companion in the depths of the Southern Ocean.

predecessors, *Fisher and Paykel* and *Steinlager 2*. This was largely due to her being some seven tons lighter than the older boats, so we were able to fly full-size spinnakers and big mizzen gennakers in 35 knots of wind. The fact that we could carry all of this sail further up the wind range meant that we had to do so if we wanted to stay in front of our maxi opposition and to foot it with the flying Whitbread 60s. It was tempting to say, 'Let's back off for a while and play it safe,' but whenever we succumbed, we found we'd lost time when the next position sched came around. Of course, we weren't alone in this compulsion to drive the boat to the edge. When the fleet arrived in Fremantle at the completion of this leg, there was no shortage of horror stories of knee-knocking rides and gear broken in high-speed wipe-outs.

After days of living on board a boat in such exhausting conditions, you start to look for anything to take your mind off the sailing. On *Endeavour* this often involved accusations of that most heinous of crimes — chocolate and biscuit theft. It had become apparent that someone was going into the food locker and taking a few biscuits out of the packet on the sly. After some detective work, it was deduced that the culprit was a member of Dalts' watch, and eventually Trev was caught red-handed. It seemed suspicious, though, that Shoebie's watch, who were without doubt the leading perpetrators in food crimes, had been doing all of the investigations.

Their credibility was soon blown away when they tried to corrupt Lowlife with contraband smuggled on board by Trae. One day when we were approaching Prince Edward Island at the midway stage of the leg, Lowlife discovered the 'Foodtown' watch eating peanut slabs and looking like cats slurping cream. Offered the remaining slab, Lowlife — quite out of character — refused it and proceeded to make public the dastardly deed. For the rest of the leg there were accusations and counter-accusations of skullduggery while 'Peanut and the Chocolate Slabs', as Shoebie's watch were referred to in the logbook, defended themselves.

The Whitbread race committee had installed Prince Edward Island as a course mark in an attempt to prevent the fleet from getting too far south. This was not a particularly successful move, because before and after rounding the island the fleet ventured as far south as it has ever gone on this leg in search of stronger winds.

As we reached into the bleak island in low overcast and 30-knot northerly winds, BC observed that Prince Edward must have been very unpopular at the time with the Queen to have such a desolate place named after him. Rounding the mark, we pulled on the canvas and ran south again. With a lead of about 65 miles over *Intrum Justitia* and 118 over *Merit Cup*, we were eager to keep the boat at full pace to preserve our hard-earned advantage. At the halfway stage of the leg, we were very happy to have built such a solid margin particularly over the Whitbread 60s, who had been relishing the heavy conditions.

Foxy's watch, with Dalts and his team on standby, enjoyed a roller-coaster ride for the next four hours with an average speed for one hour of over nineteen knots before things began to get a little hairy. A sudden squall had the boat sitting on a

Previous page: Prince Edward Island is definitely not to be recommended as a summer-cruising destination.

solid 27 knots before Foxy yelled in a less-than-controlled voice, 'Get the mizzen gennaker down — now !' Throughout that night we scorched through the darkness and by the time dawn came, everyone's nerves were stretched taut.

Shortly after dawn, a wind shift of 40 degrees made for some very tricky sailing, as the boat ran across the large seaway at an awkward angle, with each wave picking up the stern and screwing us around each time. After a brief respite, the wind increased in strength and it was decided to peel to the full-size heavy-air spinnaker to avoid blowing out the $1^1/_2$-ounce sail we were flying. Burt was hoisted up to the halyard-exit sheave to 'lock' off the halyard in order to take the weight off it and avoid chafe and possible breakages. No sooner had he reached the top of the rig when a wave slammed the boat from the leeward quarter, throwing it into a violent broach. The danger in this case is that as soon as the boat rounds up towards the wind by more than a few degrees, the massive mizzen gennaker and mizzen load up the stern, dramatically accelerating the broach.

As soon as the boat began rounding up, all Foxy could do was try to slow down the broach as the power generated by the mizzen rig spun the boat into the oncoming waves, leaving it lying on its side with the sails violently thrashing. While all this drama was happening, Burt hung on grimly at the top of the main mast, which was swinging through an arc of 10 metres.

Dalts began to lower the mizzen gennaker halyard to depower the boat and enable it to regain its footing. While the standby watch attempted to pull the massive sail on board, a wave snatched the foot and swept the sail over the stern. It became a giant sea anchor, pulling at the top of the mizzen rig and placing the mast under enormous strain. Too much strain: with a sickening graunch and metallic bang, the mast snapped clean off at the third spreaders.

As the gennaker was hauled on board, the scene on deck was as if a bomb had just gone off. Dalts stood at the base of the mizzen looking plaintively up at the broken top of the rig crashing against the remaining section and could only mutter, 'Oh no!, not the mast . . . not the mast.' Once Burt was lowered safely back down, there came the nauseating realisation that we were in very deep trouble, with 3,500 miles still to sail to Fremantle in a severely depowered boat.

A shocked crew began the depressing job of cleaning up the carnage. The first priority was to get the expensive lump of scrap metal down from the top of the stump of the mizzen. This was a very tricky operation, handled by Burt in his usual professional manner. With the broken section of mast crashing around his ears as the boat pitched and rolled in the large seaway, he spent two hours aloft with a hacksaw cutting away the thick rod stays. When the mangled rig was secured on deck, a storm spinnaker was set on the main mast and we resumed our course towards Fremantle, at a very reduced pace. The remainder of the day was spent cutting down some of the mizzen sail inventory to get what we could out of 'Stumpy', as the shortened mast became nicknamed.

From the time of the broach, no one got a moment's rest for the next 24 hours

'Stumpy' sports a drastically cut-down mizzen gennaker.

as we were immersed in the task of trying to get the mizzen working again after a fashion. It was probably the best cure for the depression we were all feeling, and kept us from dwelling on the question, 'Have we just lost the whole race because of this one broach?'

Dalts and Lowlife began to calculate how much time we were likely to lose before arriving in Fremantle, and whether it would be an insurmountable deficit for the rest of the race. BC, as always, did a great job keeping everyone positive about our prospects. His log entry about summed things up: 'Ah, what a f.....g day, first the All Blacks lose to the Poms, then our little world caved in temporarily for this leg. Who knows, there are still plenty of days left, so keep your chins up, blokes, we can still beat the bastards yet . . . , fantastic efforts all around so far.'

Trae and Moose worked like men possessed as they cut down and resewed a wide selection of sails to squeeze an extra fraction of a knot out of our wounded boat.

It soon became apparent through the scheds that we were rapidly losing our handsome lead on the fleet. We became resigned to losing time, the only question being, 'How much?'

With less than two legs of the race complete, three of the four maxi ketches in the race had broken or severely damaged their mizzen masts, and we began wondering when *Merit Cup* would join the list of casualties. Fortunately for Fehlman and his Swiss crew, they were to never join the less-than-illustrious club.

Unbelievably, three days after the broach we still led *Merit Cup* and were a good distance ahead of *La Poste*, although losing ground to both. Daniel Mallé faxed condolences, saying he did not want to beat us in this fashion. Daniel need not have worried — we had no intention of lying down and playing dead just yet.

The demolition derby continued when the youngsters on *Dolphin and Youth* were faced with a broken rudder, not a comforting prospect in the middle of the Southern Ocean. Fortunately for Matt Humphries and his multi-national crew, they were able to stop at the French meteorological base on the Kerguelen Island to build an emergency rudder to get them to Fremantle. But the woes of *Endeavour* and *Dolphin* were to prove to be little league compared with the drama that was about to unfold in the depths of a severe Southern Ocean storm in less than 24 hours time.

On a typically drab day, with constant rain and winds of 30 to 40 knots, we were blasting through the murk towards Australia when the familiar 'beep, beep, beep' of the Satcom C announced some electronic mail had just been received. Mike felt a sudden chill as he read the message from Ian Bailey Willmot, the Whitbread race director back in England, announcing that one of the Whitbread 60s, the Italian yacht *Brooksfield*, had activated its emergency EPIRB device. An EPIRB is only ever used in dire emergency, and transmits the distressed vessel's position and identification code by satellite to search and rescue authorities around the world.

Within minutes we received a similar message from Canberra asking *Endeavour* — the duty yacht for the day — to try to contact *Brooksfield* to ascertain if she was,

in fact, in distress. Mike immediately attempted to call *Brooksfield* on the SSB radio but heard only an ominous silence. Hurried fax messages were sent off to the Whitbread office and search and rescue in Canberra informing them of the situation. An immediate response asked *New Zealand Endeavour* to co-ordinate a search within the fleet.

With the nearest land 2,000 miles away, we were out of aircraft range and there was no shipping in the area, so it was up to one of the Whitbread yachts to attempt to locate *Brooksfield*. Dalts was woken from his off-watch sleep to work with Mike communicating with the other yachts in the fleet. The two nearest *Brookfield*'s last EPIRB position were *La Poste* and *Winston*. Both Daniel Mallé and Brad Butterworth agreed without hesitation to stop racing and head back into huge seas and winds that were gusting to 50 knots.

As we ploughed on through the storm-force conditions, we were all lost in private thoughts contemplating what had happened to *Brooksfield*. We hoped like hell they were all right and that it had been a false alarm, but in the conditions we were experiencing it was easy to believe that something had gone very seriously wrong and that the Italians were doomed. The prospect of them being forced to abandon the boat for life rafts or trying to hold onto an upturned hull did not bear thinking about. While *Winston* and *La Poste* turned back to look for a needle in a haystack,

Trae cranked out the overtime to cut down sails for 'Stumpy'.

the leading yachts, including *Endeavour*, were faced with massive breaking seas, screaming winds and driving sleet. But as we went into 'survival mode' for the night, *Brooksfield*'s plight was always in the back of our minds.

Shortly after midnight, with the storm at its peak, Shoebie was trying to keep the boat upright as she careered down foaming seas. On one such rapid transit down a moving mountain of water, a wave broke into the deck and washed Brad back into the windward steering wheel. The impact smashed the carbon-fibre wheel, leaving Shoebie lying on his back on the cockpit floor with the remains of the wheel still in his hands. In the darkness it took a moment for the others on watch to realise what had happened before Shoebie yelled, 'Someone grab the wheel!' There was a frantic unclipping of harnesses as the crew tried to reach the wheel down to leeward. Remarkably, the boat resisted the temptation to broach and stayed on track for the ten seconds it was driverless. To cap the night off, we tore the mainsail, cracked a winch pedestal and broke a stanchion. Shoebie's finale was a spectacular flight in his sleeping bag as the boat heeled steeply, ejecting him from his bunk. Luckily his trajectory was not interrupted by any of the beams or posts that littered the boat's interior.

After this drama, the dawn produced a steadily moderating breeze, which gave us the opportunity to repair the night's damage. Although the wind was dissipating, an enormous seaway continued to throw *Endeavour* around as if we were in a giant washing machine. Within a couple of hours, however, the good news came that *La Poste* had found *Brooksfield* and everyone was safe and well. It transpired that they had broken their rudder shaft, which in turn had started to smash a hole in the bottom of the boat. The Italians had managed to stem the flow of water by jamming a bucket wrapped in a bunk squab in the hole before the interior was completely flooded. All of their electronics had been swamped, so they had been unable to communicate their plight.

While *La Poste* escorted *Brooksfield* under emergency steering towards Fremantle, we continued racing towards the finish, losing big mileage in the lighter conditions near the West Australian coast. We were amazed to be able to hold off *Merit Cup* until we were less than 400 miles from the finish. Pierre Fehlman must have been incredibly frustrated to have been unable to put some big time on us in our under-horsepowered state. Our saving grace was the predominantly fresh reaching conditions that had prevailed from the time we broke the mast until the last few days, when the wind lightened. With sufficient breeze, we had not been too badly underpowered, despite the drastically reduced sail area on the mizzen. We were, however, losing consistently on the leading Whitbread 60s, notably *Intrum Justitia*, which had given the fleet a lesson in Southern Ocean power sailing.

After 26 days of living in wet and smelly wet-weather gear in a closed-up boat, it was a relief to encounter some warmth in the last couple of days of the marathon

(Following page) Intrum Justitia, *aka 'Silver Bullet', set a new 24-hour world record for monohulls of 425 miles en-route to winning leg two.*

from Punta del Este. Spike commented in the log that it was 'nice to see BC and Lowlife on deck, it must be getting bloody smelly down there', to which BC replied, 'This boat smells like a dog kennel.' The wet socks that had been worn for ten days and were now lying festering in the bilge made for an aroma that can only be experienced on board a Whitbread boat at the end of a long leg.

Having held *Merit Cup* off for twelve days since the mizzen had broken, we had to remind ourselves as she overtook us that we were very lucky to have lost as little time as we did. At the time of the dismasting, we had thought it likely that we could lose up to 24 hours on *Merit Cup* and the leading Whitbread 60s. To finish as close as we did was more than we could have hoped for. Our last day at sea was spent running up the coast in light to moderate tail winds, exactly the conditions we were most vulnerable in. As we approached Rottnest Island at dusk, we caught a glimpse of the Spanish Whitbread 60 *Galicia Pescanova* on the horizon ahead of us. Lawrie Smith and his pan-European team had sailed a strong race to win the leg overall from Chris Dickson's *Tokio*. The press dubbed *Intrum Justitia* the 'Silver Bullet', as they had set a new 24-hour record for a monohull of 425 miles. Even so, we had managed to keep the deficit down to 8 hours, 18 minutes behind *Intrum Justitia*, and 1 hour, 46 minutes adrift of *Merit Cup*.

As a crippled *New Zealand Endeavour* approached the finish line in Fremantle in the balmy late evening, there was a collective sigh of relief amongst the guys. The second leg through the Southern Ocean is hard enough without the added drama of breaking the mast. Not only were we still in good shape for an overall victory, we had stuck together as a team. Spike hit the nail on the head when he commented soon after stepping onto dry land, 'There's nothing like a good battle to really pull a team together.'

Push as hard as they might, the Merit Cup *crew were unable to catch us until within 400 miles of the finish.*

Leg Two: Punta del Este — Fremantle (7558 miles)

Class	Boat Name	Days	Hours	Minutes	Secs	Overall Position After Leg	Average Speed for Leg
W 60	Intrum Justitia	25	14	39	06	4	12.4
W 60	Tokio	25	16	39	36	1	12.3
W 60	Winston	25	17	28	30*	6	12.3
W 60	Yamaha	25	20	27	51	5	12.3
Maxi	Merit Cup	25	21	11	34	3	12.3
W 60	Galicia 93 Pescanova	25	22	10	19	7	12.2
Maxi	New Zealand Endeavour	25	22	57	23	2	12.2
Maxi	La Poste	26	04	56	39*	8	12.0
W 60	Hetman Sahaidachny	29	19	29	30	11	10.7
W 60	US Women's Challenge	30	01	29	42	10	10.6
W 60	Brooksfield	30	10	28	50	9	10.4
Maxi	Uruguay Natural	32	08	25	03	13	9.8
W 60	Odessa	33	01	55	27	14	9.6
W 60	Dolphin and Youth	33	19	23	25	12	9.4

* Time modified by International Jury for assisting in *Brooksfield* search

---

A badly wounded New Zealand Endeavour *with the broken mizzen mast lying on the deck and a missing steering wheel.*

CHAPTER SEVEN

Better Be Home Soon

The heat of the West Australian summer came as a welcome respite from the intense cold of the Southern Ocean. As in the last Whitbread, the stopover at the end of the second leg seemed like paradise after the rough and tumble of the previous 25 days. The cold conditions of the Southern Ocean prevented any sort of personal washing, so the showers in our Fremantle apartments took a major hammering.

While the sailors spent the next couple of days showering, sleeping and eating, the shore crew swung into action, stripping the boat down and cleaning it throughout. This was not a job for the faint-hearted, with old smelly clothes scattered throughout the boat and a month's worth of grime festering in the bilge. As soon as the clean-up was complete, attention was focused on getting 'Stumpy' out of the boat and stripping it down in preparation for the new mizzen mast's arrival.

While we had been battling through the deep latitudes of the Southern Ocean, Kev A had flown to England to organise shipping our spare mizzen to Fremantle. This necessitated the mast being cut in half for loading into a 747 cargo plane for the flight to Sydney, and Kev accompanied the rig to ensure it was not damaged or 'misplaced'. From Sydney, the two sections of mast were loaded on a truck for the three-day drive across Australia to Fremantle, where it arrived less than two days after the boat.

As the fleet trickled into the welcoming harbour at the Fremantle Sailing Club, there was no shortage of harrowing stories of destruction on the high seas. Between the tales of death-defying acts related over a cold beer at Fremantle's many bars, there was much speculation as to what sort of time compensation *Winston* and *La Poste* should get for their part in the search for *Brooksfield*. This issue was to develop into a bitter argument among some of the crews during the stopover. *Brooksfield's* arrival into Fremantle was an emotional one for the Italian crew and their families. There was some opinion expressed in certain quarters that *Brooksfield* had been too hasty in activating their EPIRB when the rudder had smashed a hole in the bottom of the boat. In the conditions they and most of the fleet were experiencing at that time, no one had the right to accuse them of raising the alarm prematurely. *Brooksfield's* skipper, Guido Maisto, had made the decision that his crew's lives were in danger and had acted accordingly. It is very easy to be full of bluff and bravado once safely on dry land, but when your boat is in grave danger of sinking in the depths of the Southern Ocean, things take on a different perspective.

Most of the fleet were pulled out of the water at the excellent facilities provided by the Fremantle Sailing Club. All had varying degrees of damage, ranging from our broken mizzen mast to major delamination on *Winston* and a broken rudder on *Dolphin and Youth*. Steve Wilson from Southern Spars in Auckland came across to help Kev A put the mizzen mast back together again and ready it for stepping into

We were hellbent on being first into Auckland, which showed on our departure from Fremantle.

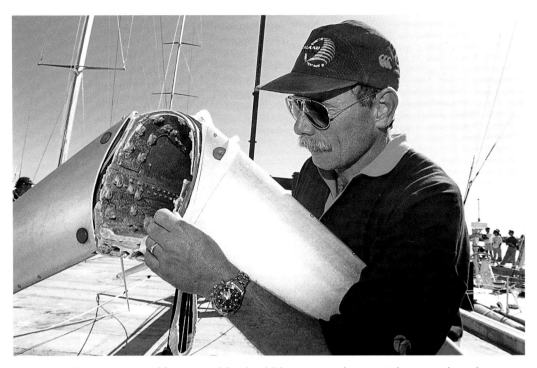

the boat. The vast paved boat yard looked like a mast farm, with more than fourteen rigs scattered around as the crews pulled them to pieces in their search for any minor defects that could result in a broken mast.

While the crews were busy repairing and servicing the yachts, there was a distinctly less congenial atmosphere among the skippers in a meeting at the Fremantle Sailing Club. Accusations had been flying for days about whether some skippers had been more willing than others to go to the stricken yacht's aid. It had all started when Dalts asked over the radio who was prepared to turn back and look for *Brooksfield*. Ross Field's response — 'We're not going back!' — was inadvertently transmitted over the SSB radio and sparked a furore. Initially, there were threats of protesting *Yamaha* for breach of sportsmanship, but no formal action was taken.

The international jury was convened to decide how much time to award *Winston* and *La Poste* in the form of redress for their part in the search for *Brooksfield*. *Winston*'s 21 hours, 28 minutes, 30 seconds moved Brad Butterworth and his team into second place for the leg, one minute behind *Intrum Justitia*. Although *Winston* had been lying in fifth place, when she turned back, in fact she had spent in excess of the time awarded bashing to windward in the storm in the search.

While all the drama was taking place in the protest room, we kept ourselves busy working on the boat in the intense Australian heat. On a couple of days the temperature hit 44 degrees, and it seemed impossible that less than 1,000 miles south

Dalts takes a closer look at the broken mizzen mast.

there were icebergs floating around. We often took a break in the middle of the day and headed off to one of Perth's spectacular white-sand beaches for a swim.

Throughout our stay in Fremantle, a local gym provided us with complementary use of their facilities, and it wasn't long before Trae, our in-house psycho fitness trainer had us up at six thirty each morning pushing weights. Our regime also included a few 'friendly' games of touch rugby, and it was good to see that even without Tony Ebert there to referee, there was no shortage of niggling and aggression. While there was some good-natured 'aggro' during our games of touch, there was no shortage of less friendly niggling among some of the other crews as numerous personnel changes began to occur. The dock was permanently seething with gossip and conjecture as the rumour mill sprang into life with stories of various people being fired.

La Poste skipper Daniel Mallé was relieved of his command after another lacklustre performance by the French maxi on leg two. There had been a lot of dissension amongst his crew over his leadership or, in their opinion, lack of it. Some of the *La Poste* crew had even taken the step of writing to the sponsors, informing them of their misgivings about Mallé's ability to win the race. His replacement was the superstar of French sailing, Eric Tabarly, who wasted no time in firing almost half of the crew and replacing them with his own people. The French campaign had started off with a hiss and a roar and enjoyed massive support. The sponsors had evidently decided that a change was needed to try to get *La Poste* at the front of the fleet and back into the headlines. Curiously, Mallé was to stay on for the remainder of the race as a regular crew member.

It came as no surprise that some of the crew on *Brooksfield* decided to quit the race. After their experiences, there were not many among us who could blame them. Somewhat more of a surprise, however, was the resignation of *Yamaha*'s navigator, Godfrey Cray. Having started the race as one of the strong favourites, Ross Field's *Yamaha* had not lived up to expectations on the first two legs. Ross had evidently come to the conclusion that they were lacking experience and expertise in the navigation and tactical department. To remedy the situation, he asked Godfrey to move on deck and called in *New Zealand Endeavour*'s original navigator, Murray Ross, to navigate on the leg to Auckland. With only a few days remaining to the restart, Godfrey decided to withdraw from the crew of *Yamaha*.

These high-profile changes were abundant proof that yachting had joined other professional sports in terms of accountability. With the huge sums of money being invested in these Whitbread campaigns, the sponsors demand a good return on their investment. In Formula One motor racing, if a driver is not performing, he is quickly fired. Whitbread yachting had suddenly joined the big league, and it was inevitable there would be some casualties.

Despite these distractions taking place around us, we remained aware that we had a very important race just ahead of us. For any Kiwi crew, leading the fleet into Auckland is almost as important as winning the race overall, and after the disappointment of our second-leg performance, we were hungry for a good result. In

the days leading up to the restart, Mike once more immersed himself in weather maps and meetings with the *Winston* brains trust, which included weather consultant Roger 'Clouds' Badham. Mike worked with the *Winston* guys before the start of each leg throughout the race, a union that seemed to pay dividends for both boats.

During the 1987 America's Cup, the 'Fremantle Doctor', as the strong south-westerly sea breeze is universally known, was legendary for its consistency. The day of the restart produced a classic appearance by the 'Doctor' that would see us start with spinnakers up for a short run up the magnificent Perth beaches, before we turned and headed upwind towards Cape Leeuwin, some 200 miles to the south. Anyone watching the start off Fremantle would have been left in no doubt that *New Zealand Endeavour* was hellbent on winning this leg as we blasted off the start line with our nose in front. By the time we dropped our spinnakers and rounded the first turning mark off Cottesloe Beach, we had a comfortable lead. The crew work on board was very smooth, which was not surprising, as we were probably more focused on winning than we had ever been.

After rounding the buoy off Cottesloe, we had a ten-mile reach across to Rottnest Island before turning for the long upwind slog towards the south-western tip of Australia. By the time we tacked onto starboard around Rottnest, *Intrum Justitia* had crossed in front of us to take the lead. In fresh conditions, the Whitbread 60s' water ballast transforms them into extremely powerful boats, but the potential drawback of

The adrenalin started pumping as soon as we crossed the start line in Fremantle and didn't stop until we finished in Auckland.

the system was graphically demonstrated as we rounded Rottnest, when Chris Dickson tacked *Tokio* just to windward of us. It rapidly became evident that the water ballast had not been fully transferred across to the new windward side, as they immediately self-tacked back, all but capsizing the boat. After Chris's comments in the media about the maxis being sailed 'badly and recklessly' during leg two, we couldn't suppress a chuckle as we watched the white hull roll onto its side.

The smiles were soon wiped off our faces though, when *Tokio* and the leading 60s blasted past us, going close to a whole knot faster. The short and steep seaway, combined with wind up to 35 knots, was making for a very uncomfortable ride. As had been the case when we left Punta a couple of months earlier, the conditions on the first day at sea made for a few queasy crew members as stomachs that had been enjoying the good life for the past month were abruptly reacquainted with life at sea.

As we pounded our way to windward, BC had to psyche himself up to get off the rail and head down into the galley. Located just behind the main mast, the galley is well forward in the boat, meaning that when *Endeavour* is leaping off waves, BC had to apply a few cowboy skills. In his words: 'Holding on is bloody hard, as my body gets twisted around and bashed at the hips on the edge of the galley. Sometimes it would be nice to have knees that swivelled 360 degrees. It is not dissimilar to trying to ride a bucking bronco with a couple of frying pans in one hand and a pot full of boiling water in the other.'

Dennis Conner helms Winston *away from Fremantle with the controversy surrounding the* Brooksfield *redress hearing still unresolved.*

While the crew on deck had a clear view of the waves ahead and could anticipate the boat's motion through the seas, BC had no such luxury buried in the bowels of the boat. After three Whitbreads in the galley, he feels he has 'developed a sixth sense, knowing when a bad wave is about to hit, through the boat's motion and my own instinct'. He aptly sums up sailing in these conditions as 'lumpy, bumpy and grumpy'.

Each time the boat fell off a big wave, BC had to hold onto the pots on top of his gas stove to prevent them from leaping into midair. It was not an uncommomn sight to see him stirring dinner with one hand while he threw up down the sink. The crew lived in fear that one day BC would misjudge his trajectory, empty his stomach into the pot of freeze-dried dinner — and they would never know the difference.

The menu that BC prepared for the race was solely freeze-dried food. Because we had no refrigeration on board, we could not carry any fresh food. By the time we arrived in port at the completion of each leg, our tolerance level for the freeze-dried gourmet delights had reached rock bottom and there was a mass exodus towards the nearest fast-food restaurant. While we were racing, an average day's menu might comprise: breakfast — cereal served with freeze-dried apples and yoghurt, mixed with powdered milk; lunch — a pasta or rice dish; and an evening meal consisting of meat dishes such as 'lamb from out of town' (Lamb Provençal), or 'beef stroke me-hoff' (Beef Stroganoff) plus dried peas, beans, corn or potatoes. All meals were served in a bowl and eaten with a fork. As there were no table or seats on board the boat, in rough conditions it would have been bordering on the impossible to try and eat a meal off a plate with a knife and fork.

The rough conditions that were BC's nemesis lasted until we rounded Cape Leeuwin on the morning after leaving Fremantle. By that time we had a five-mile lead over *Merit Cup* and *La Poste*, while the leading 60s were eight miles in front of us. It was at this stage that the first major tactical break of the leg occurred when *Winston*, with Dennis Conner on board for the leg, made a break to the south in search of stronger westerly winds. The day before the start, Roger Badham had told Mike and *Winston*'s navigator, Matteo Piazzi, that there should be a big advantage in getting south fast. *Winston* followed Roger's advice and soon found herself in a very strong position. Because we were defending our overall lead in the maxi class, we were reluctant to go off on a 'flyer' and not cover our main opposition. There was always the risk that the south would not pay off and we could get stuck out on a limb and lose our overall lead.

Even though we had moved into the lead of the boats to the north, we were becoming increasingly concerned at the rate with which *Winston* was drawing away from us. Along with the rest of the fleet, we were languishing in the light winds, while *Winston* was evidently enjoying considerably more breeze further south. By day five, *Winston* had opened up a lead of 106 miles over us. With his burning desire to be first into Auckland starting to look a little shaky, Dalts was getting increasingly edgy,

BC dishes up yet another freeze dried culinary delight.
(Inset) Feeding time at the zoo.

prompting BC to ask, 'How many pencils has he eaten?'

Our sixth morning at sea produced a dramatic increase in wind strength as the high-pressure system that had been holding us captive moved away, allowing a strong northerly flow to settle in across the Great Australian Bight. The wind arrived not a moment too soon, as *Winston*'s dream run at the head of the fleet was holding and she had extended her lead to a whopping 146 miles, making for anxiety attacks in the navigation station each time a position sched came in on the Satcom C. While we still had a very healthy margin over *Merit Cup*, we had no such edge over the vastly improved *La Poste*. Tabarly's famous hard-driving approach was obviously paying dividends and the French maxi was enjoying a new lease of life, pushing us hard every mile of the way.

Throughout the next two days we blast reached our way towards Tasmania, from where we would begin our ascent into the Tasman Sea. In the strong winds we were experiencing, we could only watch as yet again the Whitbread 60s ignited their afterburners and scorched away over the horizon. Things were starting to look a little grim at this stage, and matters became even worse when it was discovered that the chocolate had gone off and was inedible. The chocolate addicts amongst the crew were besides themselves with worry at the prospect of having to go cold turkey.

As we approached Tasmania, we were mindful of being caught in the huge island's wind shadow and decided to give it a very wide berth, passing to the south some 70 miles offshore. Even at that distance we still experienced vicious blasting squalls throughout the night as we sailed through to leeward of Tasmania. With no moon in the sky, it was impossible to differentiate between the sea and the sky, and those on watch had a very stressful time trying to anticipate the squalls. Shortly after the watch change at midnight, one such blast gave us an abrupt reminder of just who was boss. We were sailing along with a number two jib top reaching headsail, a genoa staysail inside it, full mainsail and a reefed mizzen. With this sail combination up, we were getting overpowered in the gusts and slightly underpowered in the lulls. Foxy's departing advice to Dalts at the change of watch was shouted over the roar of the wind and waves: 'It can handle more power on occasions, but watch for the big puffs!' Dalts quickly decided that we were too underpowered in the lulls and told his guys to start hoisting the small number three mizzen staysail in an attempt to generate a bit more horsepower. Unfortunately, Murphy's law dictated that no sooner had the mizzen staysail been hoisted, we were hit by a 50-knot squall with the force of a sledgehammer.

While the broach that cost us our mizzen mast had ended in catastrophe, it did not come close to the force of the one that followed very soon after the arrival of the squall. As the boat rapidly accelerated up to 23 knots, the force of the mizzen took over and spun the stern around, throwing the boat into a violent broach then leaving us pinned on our side. There was no need to call everyone on deck. The shaking and crashing of the sails telegraphed the urgency of the situation to everyone down below

and within seconds the whole crew had clambered out of the hatch into a seething maelstrom of wind-swept foam and spray. The last one on deck was Lowlife, who had been in his nav station at the time of the broach. Coming through the hatch, he said, 'Don't worry about it, guys. According to the GPS we're still going towards Auckland at six knots, even if we are on our ears!'

Even with Lowlife's comforting news, we still had major problems on our hands trying to get the boat back onto its feet again. We had to drop the mizzen staysail onto the deck, but we found that the incessant flapping had broken its battens. Next it was the turn of the mizzen to be lowered before the boat could regain its footing. There was no need to roll the genoa staysail up before lowering it to the deck, as it was now no more than a shredded Kevlar flag.

Within minutes of getting the boat up and racing again, *Intrum Justitia*'s navigation lights came into view astern of us. From the speed with which they were approaching, it was clear that Lawrie Smith and his European team were relishing the hard-running conditions. Even though we were averaging seventeen knots, she went past us as if we were anchored. The sight of a huge rooster tail erupting out from the back of their boat, illuminated by the stern light as they passed a few hundred metres to leeward of us, was spectacular. In the space of 24 hours, *Intrum Justitia* went from 24 miles behind us to 22 miles in front, sling-shotting themselves into second position in the

New Zealand Endeavour *picks up her heels on the blast across the Great Australian Bight towards Tasmania.*

process. Shortly after dawn, we received a fax, which read:

> To the Floating Pontoon,
> What took you so long? We tried to call you on the VHF last night to order your geriatric barge out of the way, but obviously you were stuck for words. We expected to hear the comforting sound of your mizzen mast crashing down last night, but evidently the reinforcing is doing its job, adding even more weight to your overloaded bulk carrier. 'Huey' might smile on you yet (out of pity), and give you your desired calms. If not, you can give us a demonstration of the reputed Kiwi 'toughness' against us European wimps in a nice beat to the finish. Come and get it!!

The *Intrum* guys should have known better than to send a message like that, as from that time on we steadily clawed back into them. As on this leg of the race four years previously, the Tasman Sea was to take control of the fleet's destiny with a major reshuffle. *Winston*'s seemingly impenetrable lead was steadily eroded as the fleet made its way north up the Tasman towards Cape Reinga. Caught by a band of high pressure that was giving them light head winds, all Dennis Conner and his crew could do was try to limit the damage as the boats behind carried a more favourable breeze up, inexorably whittling away at their lead.

With 400 miles remaining to Cape Reinga, the leading five boats were all within five miles on a radius to the top of New Zealand. *Winston* was out to the north-west of the bunch, *Yamaha* and *Intrum Justitia* were to the south-east, with *New Zealand Endeavour* and *Tokio* taking the safe option in the middle of the bunch. Moose sent a fax to *Intrum* welcoming them to Aotearoa, the land of the long white cloud. A reply was soon forthcoming, suggesting that New Zealand would be better renamed 'The land of the long black cloud, because we've been trapped under a big black cloud over here with no bloody wind!'

While *Intrum Justitia* was making slow progress towards Reinga, *Winston* was also having a tough time out on our left flank. The conservative route of sailing in the middle of the bunch was to pay dividends for *Endeavour* and *Tokio*, as we both shot out to a lead of over twenty miles. *La Poste*, who had been breathing down our necks up until this stage, also dropped off the pace, which left us to concentrate our efforts on trying to beat *Tokio* in for line honours.

We were faced with a long beat to windward in fresh air in order to reach Reinga, not exactly the conditions that maxi ketches revel in. We knew that to keep up with *Tokio* we would need to have everyone, with the exception of the four guys sleeping, on deck with their feet over the side the whole time to generate extra stability. For two days we sailed within three miles of *Tokio*, pushing the boat right to the limit. Where we would normally have changed to a smaller number three jib, we were carrying our number one genoa an extra couple of knots up the wind range to try and squeeze out that tiny extra fraction of speed. While we were sailing our boat as

The fleet ducked briefly back into the Southern Ocean *as* Merit Cup *pursued* Endeavour *and* La Poste.

well as we could, Chris and his crew were obviously doing the same and were giving no quarter. During the night before reaching Cape Reinga, *Tokio* took advantage of a wind shift to edge ahead as we tacked up along Ninety Mile Beach.

As the golden hue of the sun rising over the Northland coastline filtered across the grey Tasman Sea, we got our first glimpse of New Zealand. Any excitement we may have been feeling about seeing home for the first time in several months was countered by the sight of *Tokio* out to a lead of seven miles and about to round Reinga. By the time we reached Pandoras Bank, which separates the Pacific Ocean from the Tasman Sea off the top of New Zealand, the wind had swung around further into the east to give us a painfully slow beat across to North Cape. *Tokio* had made good use of the old breeze to lay across, spending less time tacking. It was starting to feel like whichever way we turned, things were going against us. By the time we wriggled across between the two capes, *Tokio* had done a horizon job on us, moving out to a lead of twelve miles. With less than 200 miles to the finish line in Auckland, we were starting to get more than a little twitchy.

Fortunately, once around North Cape the conditions turned in our favour, with light airs, enabling us to set up the 'arrangement', the term we used to describe our five-sail reaching configuration. Throughout the morning, the numbers of spectator boats steadily increased as we sailed down towards the Bay of Islands. There is no

The breaking dawn over Cape Reinga reveals Tokio *on the horizon ahead of us.*

other country in the world where the general public is as enthusiastic or well informed about the Whitbread as in New Zealand. It came as no surprise when we started getting calls of 'You're catching them — they're only nine miles in front now!' from people out in their boats to watch the circus roll into town.

Instead of the usual six-hourly position scheds on the Satcom C, we were now getting updates every hour, which made it easier to gauge exactly how we were going in our bid to reel in *Tokio*. By the time we sailed past Cape Brett, at the entrance to the Bay of Islands, it was starting to look as if we might just be able to catch Chris. Since rounding North Cape and setting the 'arrangement', we had enjoyed a speed edge of an extra knot over the Whitbread 60. As Skunk concentrated on steering, the three watch captains and Mike huddled in the aft cockpit debating whether we should sail inside or outside the Hen and Chicken Islands. Mike's eventual decision to take the 'high road' and go around outside the islands proved inspired. By the time we rounded the Hen and Chickens, we had ground *Tokio*'s lead down to three and a half miles.

Throughout the afternoon, Dalts was on an emotional roller coaster as the chance of winning the leg started to look tantalisingly close yet was still so far. His dream of leading the fleet into Auckland was just beyond his fingertips, and it required some amateur psychology from some of the crew to keep Dalts positive. We were all desperate to be first home, and the only way we were going to achieve that goal was to push all emotions aside and concentrate on the job at hand — racing the yacht.

On the leg across from the Hen and Chicks towards Kawau Island, we were unable to make any impression on *Tokio*'s lead. Every few minutes an anxious call of 'How are we doing?' was directed at Mike through the intercom, only to be answered with a flat reply of 'No change'. By the time we were off Kawau, we were totally dependent on radar, as we could no longer distinguish *Tokio* from the dozens of spectator boats. With 30 miles to go to the finish, Dalts took the helm and everyone moved into the positions around the deck we use for starting and finishing. With the steering wheel in his hands and a job to concentrate on, Dalts seemed to relax.

'Huey' smiled on us as we sailed past Kawau, with the wind swinging aft and enabling us to set our spinnaker and mizzen gennaker. Within minutes of setting the clouds of blue nylon sail, an excited call of 'We're starting to catch them again!' emanated from the nav station intercom. There was perceptible mood change on deck as we all realised that we still might just be able to pull it off.

For the next hour Mike kept us updated on our progress against the little green blip on his radar screen. Calls of 'We're down to 2.65 miles' were followed a few minutes later by 'Still coming in slowly, that's another 0.1 mile!' As Dalts concentrated on the red illuminated instruments on the mast, Moose helped him keep the boat in the groove, commenting, 'Good pressure in the chute there . . . No, you're a bit deep — heat it up a bit!' Trimming the spinnaker at night-time is hard enough at the best of times, and it's made no easier when there are powerful spotlights shining into your eyes. Moose had his work cut out for him trying to squint through the glare at the billowing spinnaker that was drawing us ever closer to *Tokio*.

Foxy kept an eye on *Tokio* and, communicating with Mike over the intercom, decided when to gybe as we worked our way through the narrow Tiri Passage. Once into the stretch of water off Auckland's East Coast Bays, pandemonium ensued as hundreds of spectator boats choked the inner gulf. With ten miles to go, we were still a little more than a mile behind *Tokio* and, as Mike told Phillip Leishman on Television New Zealand, we were starting to run out of highway.

As we gybed down the Rangitoto Channel, the standard of crew work was awesome. There were no raised voices, everyone knew their job inside out and, considering that every time we gybed we had to consider two mainsails and spinnakers, the speed with which we were flicking through these manoeuvres was amazing. With less then two miles to the finish, it became impossible to differentiate between the sea and the land. The harbour had been transformed into a seething mass of lights that blended into the lights all over the beaches and North Head. The constant din of clattering helicopters overhead made it almost impossible for the grinders to hear Moose's call of 'Trim!' and 'Hold!' Even though we all knew the harbour intimately, it was incredibly difficult to keep track of exactly where we were. It looked like we could have walked ashore by stepping across from boat to boat.

The sheer power being generated by our mizzen gennaker finally pulled us to within striking range of *Tokio*. We could see Chris looking over his shoulder at us with increasing intensity as we rolled up to within 200 metres. We now had to consider how we were going to pass in the narrowest part of Auckland harbour with the finish line less than a mile away. A former world match-race champion like Chris Dickson was not going to let us just sail on by. We needed plenty of water to leeward of *Tokio* if we were going to sail through between them and North Head, water that we were going to have to create by dragging our rival across towards the Rangitoto shore.

With our mizzen gennaker set, we were limited to how close to the wind we could sail before it would collapse. When *Tokio* was just a couple of boat lengths in front of us, we aimed above their stern and made it look as if we were going to try and pass them to windward. Naturally, Chris responded by heading up to counter our move. No sooner had he altered course when Mike called, 'Bear away *now*!' With the added horsepower the mizzen gennaker was producing, we were able to open up range to leeward of *Tokio*; but still not enough. Again we luffed up towards *Tokio* and once more they had no option but to try to stop us rolling over the top of them. With our bow looming within three metres of *Tokio*'s stern, Dalts once again sharply pulled away. This time we had opened up enough range between the two boats to give us the necessary space to head for the finish line, now only 500 metres away. Within a minute we knew that our tactics had paid off, as we broke through the wind shadow of the smaller Whitbread 60.

The race instructions indicated that the outer end of the finish line would be marked by a small buoy with a white flashing light. Unfortunately, the harbour was full of white lights. Now that we had managed to get our nose in front, we certainly did not want to suffer the ignominy of missing the finish line and losing the race. Even with *Tokio* now tucked away safely astern of us, we dared not relax and let down our guard — not until we'd found the damned finish line. There was a deathly silence on board as we gybed for the last time and aimed the boat through what we hoped was the line. We were oblivious to the crowds of people lining Tamaki Drive and clogging up every square metre of available harbour as we strained our eyes searching for the elusive flashing buoy.

It was not until we heard a massive cannon blast 200 metres away that we knew we had crossed the line. The scene that erupted on the deck of *New Zealand Endeavour* was fuelled by intense relief. Kiwi yachtsmen are known around the world for their lack of emotional displays when winning races, but this occasion was an exception. We all jumped up and down, waving our arms around like lunatics and yelling at the top of our voices. The emotional wave that swept over the boat was every bit as powerful as a huge Southern Ocean swell. Judging from the celebrations erupting around us, it was clear that there were a lot of New Zealanders that were equally pleased to see us home first. The trip up the Waitemata Harbour was chaotic, with an armada escorting us up towards the Heineken Village. Entering the Viaduct Basin to the cheers of a crowd of 30,000 was nothing short of overwhelming. Trae summed our feelings up when he said '*This* is why we do the Whitbread race!'

An overwhelming sense of relief engulfed us as we crossed the finish line.

The sight of people hanging off street signs and anything else that afforded a good view was unbelievable. The roaring chant of 'Kiwis! Kiwis! Kiwis!' all but drowned out the sound of the National Anthem being played at full volume over the PA system. By the time we had tied up alongside the arrival pontoon, our faces were set in permanent grins.

As soon as the Heineken Trophy presentation was completed, we moved *New Zealand Endeavour* off the pontoon to make room for Chris to bring *Tokio* alongside. We all stood on the foredeck of *Endeavour* to applaud Chris and his team for an excellent job winning the Whitbread 60 class. Within a space of a few minutes we were wondering why we had bothered as we listened to Chris sink his teeth into us on television. But it was going to take a lot more than Chris's comments to ruin the celebration we were having with our families and friends. It felt great to be home!

The welcome we received at the Viaduct Basin was an experience none of the crew will ever forget.

Leg Three: Fremantle — Auckland (3272 miles)

Class	Boat Name	Days	Hours	Minutes	Secs	Overall Position After Leg 3	Average Speed for Leg
Maxi	*New Zealand Endeavour*	13	08	15	45	2	10.2
W 60	*Tokio*	13	08	17	57	1	10.2
W 60	*Winston*	13	10	57	54	5	10.1
W 60	*Yamaha*	13	11	07	59	3	10.1
Maxi	*La Poste*	13	11	35	27	8	10.1
W 60	*Galicia 93 Pescanova*	13	11	35	39	6	10.1
W 60	*Intrum Justitia*	13	13	15	02	7	10.0
Maxi	*Merit Cup*	13	16	26	04	4	9.9
W 60	*Dolphin and Youth*	13	18	10	55	12	9.9
W 60	*Brooksfield*	13	22	04	57	9	9.8
W 60	*Heineken*	14	00	08	10	10	9.7
W 60	*Hetman Sahaidachny*	15	10	53	10	11	8.8
Maxi	*Uruguay Natural*	16	19	36	53	13	8.1
W 60	*Odessa*	16	21	07	38	14	8.0

Dalts hoists aloft the Heineken Trophy.

CHAPTER EIGHT

Living on the Edge

After the arrival of *New Zealand Endeavour* and *Tokio* in Auckland, the party continued on through the night as the rest of the fleet trickled into the Viaduct Basin. Each boat received huge support from the crowd of spectators, many of whom stayed until dawn.

Chris Dickson's comments on arrival had stirred the embers of controversy and the media quickly fuelled the fire. Virtually everyone in New Zealand, it seemed, had an opinion on the incident and throughout the next day reactions to it were broadcast hourly on the radio stations. Once the dust had settled a bit and we had the chance to take it all in, we were amazed to hear exactly what had been said.

Chris suggested that if the *New Zealand Endeavour* crew 'had been sailing a 60, they wouldn't have been here for another half-day or so. Tactically, and sailing the boat, they didn't do as well as they should have done. I'm sure they're not very happy with themselves, but they don't need us to tell them that.' In fact we were pretty happy. We had convincingly won the Heineken Trophy for the maxi class, and had led the fleet into our home port. It goes without saying that we didn't sail the perfect race, no one ever has, but it did sting to have these comments levelled at us at the end of what had proved to be a very demanding leg.

Throughout the race, the maxi versus Whitbread 60 debate had been simmering on the back burner; finally the heat had been turned right up. It had been the intention of the Whitbread race committee to have the maxis faster, but it was not turning out that way. The 60s' performance capabilities had been underestimated by everyone, including their designers. By way of comparison, the maxis could be described as big, heavy V8s, with the Whitbread 60s being a smaller but turbo-charged car. At the end of the day, each had strong suits and they ended up going around the circuit at very similar speeds. By the time the race was to finish, many of the *New Zealand Endeavour* crew had become frustrated at what they saw as a 'no win' situation. On the legs when we beat the 60s, it was fully expected because we were 'so much bigger, with more sail area'. But when a Whitbread 60 beat us, or came close as had just happened, we 'obviously weren't sailing the boat very well'.

The day after our arrival, Chris phoned Dalts and apologised, saying that he had woken that morning regretting his press conference outburst. He then went on national television and radio and blamed his statements on tension and tiredness. We were all pleased when Chris cleared the air. It must have taken some guts to publicly retract everything, and his action stilled the troubled waters.

All of the overseas crews were very impressed with facilities at the Heineken Village, where the boats were moored, and with the massive levels of interest being shown towards the race by the New Zealand public. With the possible exception of France, there is no other country in the world where people are as well educated or

Peeling mizzen staysails as we round Coromandel Peninsula.

enthusiastic about yachting. Everyone involved with the Viaduct development and race organisation in Auckland should have felt justifiably proud of their efforts.

With a couple of exceptions, all of the boats were hauled out of the water for repairs and maintenance during the stopover to ready them for their next appointment with the Southern Ocean. *New Zealand Endeavour* underwent an extensive refit, as we serviced every aspect of the boat to ensure she would make it halfway around the world back to England. The relatively low cost of getting work done, and the ease with which we could organise everything, made our extensive programme fairly straightforward. For the *Merit Cup* crew, however, things were not quite as simple. Upon hauling their boat out of the water, they discovered a large section of the lead had fallen off the steel frame within the keel. Fortunately for the Swiss, they were able to get this mishap repaired with minimal fuss. They would have been in much more trouble had they tried to do the same job in Punta del Este.

One of the highlights of the stopover for us was an exhibition race between the *Endeavour* crew and Russell Coutts and his 'Team New Zealand' America's Cup crew, aboard *NZL 10* and *NZL 12*. Prior to the race on Auckland's Anniversary Day, Russell had told us, 'We'll take it easy, we don't want to get into any pre-start manoeuvres that might damage the boats.' Those of us that knew Russell's fierce competitiveness took his assurances with a grain of salt, and in the last couple of minutes before the start we were proved correct, as Russell quickly had us on the ropes. Once we had extracted ourselves, we managed to hang onto them for the remainder of the race, losing by just a minute in what was a most enjoyable diversion from the Whitbread.

In keeping with the trend that had started in Punta del Este, the hirings and firings amongst the fleet continued in Auckland. The first casualty was *Tokio*'s watch captain, Joe English, who left the campaign 'for personal reasons'. The rumours in the waterfront bars had it that English, who had skippered *NCB Ireland* in the previous Whitbread, had been given an adverse performance review and was asked to leave. With less than two days to the restart, *Intrum Justitia*'s watch captain, Gunnar Krantz, was issued with a one-way plane ticket home from Lawrie Smith on the basis that they didn't get on very well. Krantz's replacement was Marco Constant, who sailed on *Atlantic Privateer* in the 1985/86 Whitbread and happened to be in Auckland at this time.

The final high profile crew change came with the recruitment of Nik White as navigator on *Yamaha*. In what was to prove to be a race-winning move, Ross Field hired the Wellington meteorologist to work with him in the navigation station for the remainder of the race. Meanwhile, former *Yamaha* navigator Godfrey Cray joined *Winston*. The Whitbread race was fast developing into a game of 'musical boats'.

As we had done prior to the start of each previous leg, the watch captains met with Mike Quilter on the day before the restart to formulate a game plan. On this occasion, Mike had very firm views on how best to tackle this leg of the race. From a tactical perspective, it could be broken into two halves: the trip across the Southern Ocean to Cape Horn, and then the 1400 miles up the Atlantic Ocean to Punta.

Based on valuable experience gained in the last two Whitbread races, Mike had drawn up a list of do's and don'ts. In his pre-race briefing to the crew, Mike quipped, only half in jest, 'We're not going below 60 degrees South unless everyone has brought a signed note from their mother.' Behind Mike's humour was a strong resolve to stick to his plan of never sailing below the 'no-go' latitude of 60 degrees. This was not because it was too cold down there, but rather any boat that ventured beneath this latitude ultimately rounded the Horn in poor shape. This race was to prove to be no exception.

The start day dawned with a blustery north-easterly wind blowing across the Waitemata Harbour, accompanied by heavy, squally showers. The hectic schedule we had encountered in Auckland saw many of the crew stepping on board the boat in need of a rest, but one look up the harbour at the windswept water convinced us that we were heading into the wrong environment. Even though we knew we were only halfway through the job at hand, no one was keen to be leaving friends and family again after a month at home. With very mixed feelings, we slipped our dock lines and headed out into the harbour to prepare for the start.

It seemed that the rest of the fleet were more than ready to leave town, judging by a stampede on the start line that resulted in eight boats being recalled for starting prematurely. Fortunately, Burt was on the ball and called us right onto the line, leaving

The Waitemata Harbour was transformed into a washing machine as the Whitbread fleet left town.

us with a clean getaway out of the harbour, while the bulk of the fleet had to turn back. By the time we reached the turning mark off Mairangi Bay, Chris Dickson had *Tokio* out into a comfortable lead over *Yamaha*, who in turn beat us to the mark by eleven seconds. Memories of *The Card* losing her mizzen mast among the spectator fleet leaving Auckland in the last race encouraged a conservative approach on board *Endeavour*.

The windy conditions we experienced leaving Auckland were to be an omen of what lay in wait for us over the next few days as we began our rapid descent into the Southern Ocean down past the Chatham Islands. By dawn on the day after the start, the leaders were off East Cape, which was living up to its reputation as an unpleasant place to go yachting. With all of the hatches closed to try and keep the boat relatively dry, the interior of the boat was becoming very stuffy, which, combined with the rough ride we were experiencing, made for some tender stomachs.

Over the next three days, the fleet scorched southwards past the Chatham Islands on the great circle course towards the Horn. We watched with fascinated interest as *La Poste* headed directly towards the Chathams. While the rest of the fleet had decided early on which side they were going to pass the islands, Tabarly appeared to be heading directly for them. It was only when they got within twenty miles of the rugged islands that they altered course. It transpired that the navigator had been using French electronic charts, which did not show the Chathams at all, and it was only when they saw the islands on the horizon that they became aware of their existence.

By the time we began our third day at sea, the leading Whitbread 60s were out to a strong lead of over 70 miles — definitely not the most encouraging way for us to start the fourth leg. We had the consolation of leading the maxis from a much-improved *Merit Cup*. Soon after passing the Chathams, we crossed the international date line, thus gaining a day. It was suggested in the logbook that as it was Brad's turn to clean the head that day, he should have to do it again tomorrow. Agreement was unanimous — it was entirely appropriate that Brad, the most prolific user of the head, should have to clean it two days in a row.

More seriously, at the midnight change of watch soon after crossing the date line, Foxy felt a strong vibration coming through the steering wheel. Hanging over the side of the boat and armed with a torch, Sean discovered a large plastic bag wrapped around the leading edge of the rudder. No amount of 'flossing' with a batten and rope could free the obstinate garbage off the rudder, and eventually Sean climbed into the dry suit and was lowered over the side of the boat on a halyard for a high-speed midnight dip in the frigid water. Even then he couldn't get rid of the source of the vibration, and after a couple of hours of trying there was no option but to back up.

Backing up an America's Cup yacht in the light winds off San Diego is one thing, but backing a maxi up in 25 knots of wind in the middle of the night with a big sea running is an altogether different proposition. At the watch change we lowered the

mizzen and jib top, and spun into the wind to stop the boat. Within seconds, the wind and waves pushed the boat backwards, freeing the plastic bag, and we were able to rehoist the mizzen and jib top and resume racing again. Our contest with *Merit Cup* was so close that the mile we lost in this manoeuvre was reflected in the next position sched.

On the fifth day at sea, we were beginning to have grave concerns about our position relative to the rest of the fleet. *Endeavour* and *Merit Cup* were the northern-most boats at 52 degrees, while many of the 60s had dived south aggressively and were now more than 100 miles below. Mike was hopeful that a ridge of high pressure would ensnare the boats in the south, leaving us with more wind. Whatever happened, our bed had been made and we were going to have to lie in it and hope.

Later that day, a steady freshening in the breeze soon had us flying across the steely-grey sea at breakneck speed with a full-size spinnaker and mizzen gennaker set. After a smoking six-hour run of 105 miles, Mike burst out of the aft hatch with an ear-to-ear grin: 'We're dorking them — we've put 50 miles on the leading 60s!'

For years Dalts had been obsessed with breaking through the 400-mile barrier for a 24-hour run. Although the Whitbread 60s were able to breach this threshold almost at will, on a 27,000-kilogram maxi it is a more difficult proposition. Dalts' ambition was realised as we streaked into the lead, while the bulk of the fleet

Radio interviews back to New Zealand were part of Dalt's daily schedule.

languished in lighter airs over the horizon to the south of us. To 'crack the 400', we needed perfect conditions — steady 30 to 40-knot winds and big waves to keep us surfing. We eventually managed a run of 405 miles, an average of 16.9 knots over 24 hours.

During this period of solid surfing, we broached in the middle of the night with a full-size spinnaker and mizzen gennaker set. Nightmares of the similar broach during leg two, which resulted in a broken rig, flashed through our minds as the sheer power of the mizzen rig took control of the boat. The lessons learnt from the mast-breaking incident were put to use in the form of a 'panic release' for the mizzen gennaker. By 'spiking' away the sparcraft clip on the tack of the mizzen gennaker, we were quickly able to bring both the gennaker and the boat back under control. As the gennaker tack was tripped, the enormous load on the clip created an immense spark that illuminated the whole cockpit.

Just as we were settling into the increased tempo of sailing downwind in the heavy conditions, the centre of the low-pressure system that had provided us with the fresh winds passed over and left us completely becalmed. Sitting in the freezing cold drizzle, all we could do was try and prevent damage as the left-over seaway threw the boat around like a cork. With no wind to steady the sails, the booms thrashed

Sean has the boat percolating on our dash to the Horn.

from side to side with metallic crashes, and the constant slapping of the Kevlar sails was almost deafening. Our concern was relieved at the next sched, when it became apparent that we were not alone in the parking lot and our lead was still intact.

Within hours the breeze began to build from the north-east, leaving us with head winds on our course towards Cape Horn. There is only one thing worse than being on the wind, and that's being on the wind in the Southern Ocean. The cold that is merely uncomfortable when you're running with the wind becomes extremely unpleasant as the boat crashes its way into a large and confused seaway and the wind speed across the deck approaches 50 knots.

The amount of clothes worn in these conditions is enough to make even the smallest person take on the appearance of the Michelin Man. From the time one of the on-watch crew wakes you from a deep sleep, with water dripping off his sodden jacket onto your forehead, it takes twenty minutes to get dressed. Most of us slept in a pair of polypropylene long johns and thermal socks. The first item of clothing pulled on once out of the warmth of the sleeping bag is a thick thermal pullover. Next comes the middle layer, consisting of fleece-lined pants and jacket with a nylon shell on the exterior. By now, your body is starting to warm up and it's time to pull on the thick rubber sea boots.

Sailing upwind in the Southern Ocean is no one's idea of fun.

With no large drying locker on board *New Zealand Endeavour*, our gear was constantly damp and it's never fun pulling on sodden wet-weather pants and jacket over the top of everything else. The final step of getting dressed for work was to pull on a pair of gloves and a hat, and clip on the safety harness. At this stage we had to hope that nature didn't call — it was a major exercise in dexterity and perseverance to work through five zips and countless flaps to get down to business.

Life on board a Whitbread boat can be an object lesson in balance and timing. During lunch one day, Nick discovered the effect gravity can have on one's equilibrium if caught unaware. While he was exiting the galley with a bowl of BC's finest chilli con carne, the boat leapt off a particularly big wave and Nick's meal went flying through the air, liberally spraying all over the deck head. BC thought it was a huge joke until it became apparent that the bulk of Nick's lunch had been deposited on his jacket, lying beside the galley.

A reprieve from life on the wind came on the last few days prior to rounding Cape Horn, when the wind swung into the north to give us a blast reach. Sailing beam-on to the sea can be a bit tricky on occasions, particularly when a rogue wave decided to break onto the deck. It was just as well Burt was adept at repairing steering wheels, because he got another opportunity to demonstrate his skill after a large wave washed him off the helm onto the cockpit floor with a severely mangled wheel still in his hands. The same wave washed Hermie four metres down the deck, and only the weather satellite aerial prevented him from carrying on straight over the stern.

With the Horn less than 1000 miles away, we were enjoying a lead of 106 miles over *Tokio*. An incredibly complex series of low-pressure systems, with no fewer than seven centres, was making for a navigator's nightmare as Mike tried to plot a course through the minefield. At one stage our barometer bottomed out at 960 hPa, lower than any of us had ever experienced before. While we sat virtually becalmed for more than a day, *Tokio* sailed on through to a lead of 25 miles in less than 48 hours. It was pretty depressing to see twelve days' effort evaporate so quickly.

We need not have been too concerned, however, as the game of chance was to continue all the way to Cape Horn. The weather patterns were creating 'rivers' of wind that were often only 30 miles wide, making for massive and abrupt gains and losses within the fleet. Fortunately for us, Mike's resolve to stick to his plan of staying above 60 degrees South paid dividends and we arrived at the Horn in good shape only nine miles astern of *Intrum Justitia*. The Europeans on the 'Silver Bullet' had once more proved that they were the masters of Southern Ocean sailing, breaking their own 24-hour distance record with a run of 428.7 miles.

While *Tokio* and *Galicia* had been looking dangerous on the chart, when it came time for them to ascend out of the sub-60 latitudes, they lost out by having to sail on the wind while the boats further to the north reached in. They eventually rounded the Horn astern of *Yamaha* and some 45 miles behind *New Zealand Endeavour*.

As we rounded in relatively placid weather, the veterans among the crew reflected that they had never sailed around this infamous landmark in more than

twenty knots of wind. The stories of severe gales and countless lives lost seemed unlikely, but the wrecks that adorn the shores of the Cape proved the possibility of disaster. If sailing around the Horn was a low-stress event, the pilot of a Chilean naval helicopter seemed intent on trying to liven things up for us. We were more than a little anxious as the chopper went through a series of death-defying aerobatic stunts within metres of our rig, behaving like a demented blowfly.

The Strait de le Maire always gives the Whitbread fleet a thumping. It separates the might of the Southern and Atlantic Oceans, and experiences tremendous tidal streams. When these oppose the wind, large seas build up, making for a very quick and bumpy transit into the Atlantic. But, after this brief roller-coaster there was a perceptible change in mood on board *Endeavour* as we turned the corner and headed north. Now, every day would bring a welcome increase in the air temperature.

With 1400 miles to the finish, *Intrum Justitia* was going to take a lot of catching, judging by the weather-fax maps that indicated we were in for several days of head winds. As we set off in pursuit of the Euros, we had the standby watch sitting on the

We often felt scuba gear would be useful on deck.

windward rail, trying to coerce every fraction of speed out of the boat. After four hours of being 'rail meat', things could become boring and we would often keep ourselves amused with trivia quizzes. When it came to television questions, the generation gap among the crew became evident, with the older members being experts on shows such as *Get Smart* and *Charlie's Angels*, while the fresher-faced proved to have all the answers on *Bay Watch* and *Beverly Hills 90210*.

Things began to go our way when the wind swung into the west, enabling us to ease sheets and set up our five-sail reaching 'arrangement' for the first time in a few days. Even though we were 150 miles off the Argentine coast, the dust blowing from the Pampas plains enshrouded the whole boat in a thin film of black dirt. For Dalts, a stickler for cleanliness, this was close to his worse nightmare. However, even if the boat was filthy, we were still managing to grind *Intrum Justitia* down. Soon after passing through the Strait de le Maire, she had jumped out to a lead to 40 miles.

One thing we did become very adept at on *Endeavour* was catching the opposition. With 500 miles to the finish line in Punta, 'Huey' smiled on us and trapped *Intrum Justitia* in a cell of high pressure, and it was not long before we spotted the silver Whitbread 60 on the horizon abeam of us. Understandably, Lawrie Smith was unhappy with this development and wasted no time in sending us a fax:

> To the Great White Slug
> What took you so long? We've been sitting here becalmed and it's taken you days to catch up to us. Your boat, with twice the sail area, twice the budget and quarter of our salary bill, just doesn't seem to be able to get out of its own way. When you guys get your conditions, it takes you days to make even the smallest gain on us. See you in Punta!

Considering that in the previous leg the guys on *Intrum* had been badly burnt when they sent us a similar fax, we were surprised that they didn't know better. Mike couldn't resist a bit of stirring and immediately replied:

> To the Silver Suppository
> What are you guys still doing here? We would've thought that having enjoyed no less than fifteen days of perfect 60s' weather getting to the Horn, you would have been in Punta by now flopping a few cold ones. What have you been doing?

With this light repartee, the stage was set for a sprint to the finish. For the next three days, if you were not off watch, it was a case of bums on the rail. In many respects, it was a very similar scenario to that encountered racing *Tokio* up the Tasman Sea a few weeks previously. The radar was monitored regularly to gauge our progress against *Intrum*, and it became a nerve-racking task trying to keep them behind us. Had it been *Tokio* or *Yamaha* on our tail, it is debatable as to whether we could have held them off. The power of the Whitbread 60 was very hard to defend against, as they could inherently point a degree or two higher than us while sailing to windward.

New Zealand Endeavour *rounds the infamous Cape Horn hot on the heels of* Intrum Justitia.

During our last day at sea, *Intrum* closed to within half a mile of us, and it was very much a case of the finish into Auckland scenario in reverse. The question was, could we hold them off over the last 30 miles?

As we closed on the finish, Mike took a bearing across the deck and announced, 'We can't cross them, they're in front.' It was going to be pretty hard to swallow losing the race for line honours after such a tough leg, but with ten miles to go anything could happen. And it did. *Intrum Justitia* tacked away from the controlling position and gave us another life. Mike was convinced that sailing right in close to the shore was the only way to go, so we held our breath as Smith tacked *Intrum* away back out to sea again. All we could do was be patient as Foxy concentrated on driving the boat, while Moose, Brad and Trae nursed every fraction of a knot of boat speed out of the sails. Finally, Mike said, 'Let's tack now. We're almost on the lay-line.'

It is amazing how your eyes can play tricks at night-time when looking for a faint light in the distance. After numerous false sightings, we spotted the red navigation light on *Intrum*'s bow and immediately wondered who was going to cross in front. As the boats slowly converged, it became apparent that the inshore road was the winner and we had a half-mile advantage. With two miles to go, we took no chances and tacked to windward of them in a loose covering position, making sure we followed the basic rule of staying between the opposition and the finish line.

By the time *New Zealand Endeavour* got the gun, *Intrum* had disappeared back into the darkness and ended up crossing the line five minutes and 39 seconds behind us. Things were obviously looking up; our winning margins were on the increase again after our two-minute twelve-second win into Auckland. We seemed to be

Grinding the spinnaker sheet was a full-time job.

making a habit of these nail-biting finishes in the middle of the night, and our relatively comfortable win on leg one was only a fond memory.

Waiting on the arrival barge to catch our dock lines were the members of our trusty shore crew. While we had been racing across the Southern Ocean, they had been keeping in touch with us by fax to ensure that any necessary spares were brought to Uruguay. While for the sailing team the work was over for a couple of days, for the shore crew it was just beginning.

Even with a hard slog ahead of them on the following day, the shore crew were always right in the thick of the arrival celebrations. We marvelled at their capacity for partying and then getting up for work a few hours later. The end of each leg was always a festive occasion, with a reunion between the sailing and the shore crews and, most importantly, with our long-suffering wives and girlfriends.

As the celebrations on board *Endeavour* increased in tempo, we were all highly amused when Smith launched into one of his characteristic whinges as soon as he docked in Punta. His comments that we had 'tacked on them five or six times' were way off the mark, and he then went on to claim that we were just a nuisance and had got in their way. The solution to that problem should have quickly occurred to someone who believes in his own talents as much as Lawrie does — get in front and stay in front!

Leg Four: Auckland — Punta del Este (5914 miles)

Class	Boat Name	Days	Hours	Minutes	Secs	Overall Position After Leg	Average Speed for Leg
Maxi	*New Zealand Endeavour*	21	02	26	13	1	11.6
W 60	*Intrum Justitia*	21	02	31	52	3	11.6
Maxi	*Merit Cup*	21	06	45	55	4	11.5
W 60	*Tokio*	21	07	29	06	2	11.5
W 60	*Yamaha*	21	07	37	33	5	11.5
W 60	*Galicia 93 Pescanova*	21	10	38	21	6	11.4
Maxi	*La Poste*	21	13	35	14	8	11.3
W 60	*Winston*	22	02	26	24	7	11.1
W 60	*Brooksfield*	22	05	47	57	9	11.0
W 60	*Heineken*	22	13	51	52	10	10.8
W 60	*Dolphin and Youth*	22	17	21	37	11	10.7
W 60	*Hetman Sahaidachny*	22	22	21	52	12	10.7
Maxi	*Uruguay Natural*	24	18	41	41	13	9.9
W 60	*Odessa*	24	21	37	14	14	9.8

CHAPTER NINE

Who Wrote the Script?

Throughout the race, we hosted several parties on board *New Zealand Endeavour* at the end-of-leg festivities, and we were always joined by the crews of the boats that had finished just in front or behind us. The Uruguayans looked on with amusement as the *Intrum Justitia* team came on board for a few drinks and the pace of the party rapidly escalated. Even Lawrie Smith joined in, which struck some of us as being a bit cheeky considering the comments he had just made to the assembled media. Smith defended these, saying that he had been trying to generate some publicity for his sponsors and didn't really mean the criticism. Most of us had trouble swallowing that excuse.

Throughout the night boats filtered into Punta and, within minutes of docking, the crews headed straight for the local watering hole, Moby Dick's. After the rigours of the Southern Ocean, many of the crews were hell-bent on unwinding, and it didn't take long for Moby Dick's to become a seething mass of inebriated yachtsmen. The intensity of the party was such that it was fortunate we were in Uruguay, where the police and bar-owners take a relaxed view towards spirited partying. While enjoying a few drinks with his crew, Chris Dickson managed to fall off a table top and ended up being carted off to hospital in a neck brace with a serious concussion.

Most of the fleet arrived in Punta with minimal damage, with the noticeable exception of *Dolphin and Youth* and *Heineken*. For Matt Humphries and his young crew, it was a relief to arrive in Punta, having sailed for 2500 miles with several broken bolts on their keel, which could have snapped off at any time. The women on *Heineken* completed the leg with a broken rudder. Unfortunately for Dawn Riley and her crew, this was to become a recurring problem.

While Punta del Este had been bordering on a ghost town during our first stopover, several months earlier, this time the resort was considerably busier with thousands of South American holiday-makers enjoying themselves. Consequently, everything was even more expensive than it had been on our previous visit — a movie ticket cost up to $25.

One very popular entertainment was the 'Punta Olympics', comprising tennis, swimming, running, volleyball, a tug of war, and the premier event — the big-splash competition off the high board. Held at a nearby country club, the multinational olympics offered typically fierce competition, and it was obvious that there were some incredibly talented sportsmen among the Whitbread crews. At the conclusion of the day, the *New Zealand Endeavour* team came out on top, amidst much finger-pointing and accusations of skullduggery from some of the other competitors.

A more sombre mood was to envelop everyone involved with the Whitbread race as a result of a burglary in the *La Poste* crew house. Unfortunately, it seemed to be a fact of life that we would have either personal or boat equipment stolen during

Nick clips the mizzen staysail on ready for hoisting.

the Punta stopover. On both our visits with *New Zealand Endeavour*, most of us had clothing stolen.

It was not too surprising, then, that two burglars were discovered in the process of ripping off the French house. One of them managed to escape with a couple of wallets, but the other one was apprehended. The incensed Frenchmen took it upon themselves to 'encourage' him to reveal where their stolen wallets could be found. The thief refused to co-operate and bore the brunt of his captors' frustration.

The *La Poste* crewmen eventually called the local police to have the burglar arrested, but once the Uruguayan burglar had told his story, it was the Frenchmen who were charged with assault and deprivation of liberty. While they became guests of the Uruguayan government, the burglar was released with a warning and had his initials printed in the newspaper. Although the *La Poste* guys had obviously overstepped the mark, we could all understand their reaction to the burglary. Despite high-level negotiations, nothing could be done to free the imprisoned sailors and, with the restart looming, it appeared that Eric Tabarly was going to be short of four crew members.

There was considerable tension in Punta following this incident and much relief when the day of the restart arrived and we were able to get back out racing again. As *La Poste* headed out to the start line, her reduced crew formed a line along the rail to spell the word LIBERTAD with their shirts as a show of solidarity. With no trial date set, there was no telling how long their compatriots would remain incarcerated.

At the Punta del Este restart, the La Poste crew show solidarity for their imprisoned crewmates left behind in a Uruguayan jail.

It was off the coastline of Punta del Este that the Battle of the River Plate had taken place during the Second World War. In memory of the New Zealand servicemen that lost their lives, Dalts performed a brief service before casting a wreath into the waters of the river. We felt sure that those men would have been pleased that a new generation of New Zealanders were remembering them as they prepared for their own battle.

Almost every crew in the fleet had attempted to lighten their boats for what was expected to be a cake walk in light winds. Anything that was not considered absolutely essential was removed from the boat. This included a lot of the spares and repair kits that are so essential on the Southern Ocean legs, but within a few days many were wishing they had not been quite as ruthless in this culling.

A combination of light winds and a good start saw *New Zealand Endeavour* lead the fleet away from Punta del Este, closely followed by *Merit Cup* and *La Poste*. So far the script was as anticipated; on paper, if ever a maxi was likely to win a leg, this was the one. Nightfall saw the fleet rock-hopping along the coast in an effort to elude the adverse Brazilian current. Throughout the first night at sea the boats moved *en masse*, with no one wanting to take any chances by breaking away from the bunch.

For the next three days, unusually persistent and large wind shifts of up to 40 degrees kept us tacking at regular intervals as we tried to stay 'in phase'. For the off watch this became increasingly frustrating, as it resulted in very broken sleep as the call came down the hatch: 'Change sides!' The leading bunch of Whitbread 60s, *Tokio*, *Yamaha* and *Intrum Justitia*, were setting the pace twenty miles ahead, while

Just before the Punta restart, Dalts performed a brief memorial ceremony for the New Zealand veterans of the Battle of the River Plate.

the three ketches remained in a tight huddle.

After nearly a week at sea we had not once been able to lay course towards the north-eastern corner of Brazil, and our progress across the chart was depressingly slow. Any misconceptions we had been harbouring about the weather we should experience on this leg were dispelled when the wind and the seas steadily began to increase. Life below decks became unpleasant, as the big seas continually washing along the deck meant the hatches were permanently shut and the interior was exceedingly hot and sticky.

The fifth day of the leg is one that Chris Dickson and his *Tokio* crew are unlikely to forget. While sailing upwind under full mainsail and a number three genoa in 25 knots of air, *Tokio* suddenly sat upright. The mast had snapped clean in half just above the first set of spreaders, and with it went any hope of *Tokio* winning the Heineken Trophy. For Chris and his team, it must have been totally devastating to watch two years of planning come tumbling down with their rig. No one wishes that sort of bad lucky on anyone, and, based on our leg-two dismasting, we could imagine how depressed they must have felt. At least when our mizzen broke, we were able to continue racing with our main mast.

A breaking wave has New Zealand Endeavour's *name written all over it. . .*

Within hours of *Tokio*'s departure from the front row of the grid, the hapless *Dolphin and Youth* crew discovered that large sections of their hull had delaminated. With no sign of the boat-breaking sea conditions abating, Matt Humphries made the decision to slow down and head for Rio de Janeiro to repair the damaged section of hull. The conditions were wreaking havoc through the whole fleet, and it seemed that at each position sched another story of woe and destruction was relayed over the radio.

New Zealand Endeavour was soon to join the casualty list. Dawn on our sixth day at sea revealed another horizon of breaking seas and windswept skies. As the wind strength climbed to 40 knots, the outboard reefing line snapped, permitting the unrestrained Kevlar sail to thrash violently. To prevent the sail from destroying itself, we quickly lowered it while Spike spliced up a new reefing line down below. With no mainsail up to support the top of the mast, the tapered top section of the rig was whipping around and, as the boat lunged off a wave, the all-important masthead wind gear snapped clean off. Until the conditions moderated enough to enable us to replace the carbon-fibre wand with our spare one, we would be sailing 'blind', as the wind gear was a critical element in the boat's electronic instrumentation.

. . .moments later a wall of water is thrown skyward as the wave slams the hull.

The situation was about to worsen as we continued bumping our way to windward through the steep seas. While making a drink, Moose sensed a disturbing grinding noise coming from the hull beside the galley. Bending down, he heard the unmistakable sound of the Nomex honeycomb core grinding and starting to break up. If the sound alone was not enough to alarm him, the sight of the hull flexing by 100 millimetres certainly was. Dalts was quickly summoned to check the situation out and immediately the comment 'Bear away now!' was issued to the on-watch crew. To avoid further structural damage, we had to turn downwind to prevent the boat from pounding into the waves. With *Merit Cup* only two miles ahead of us, it was frustrating to have to turn away from the chase.

For the next three hours, temporary repairs were made to the hull to enable us to head back on course again, albeit at a reduced tempo. To prevent the core from further failure, floor boards were cut up and placed against the affected section of hull. The only props that were long enough to reach from the hull up to the deck head were bunk frames. Before they knew what was going on, Mike and BC found themselves homeless as their bunks were sacrificed for the repair. Even some of Mike's pilot books were used as chocks.

Curiously, just over the horizon, *La Poste* was about to suffer the same problem. Very few boats were to escape the rough conditions without some sort of gear or laminate failures, and these intensified the debate as to whether tougher rules should be imposed to guarantee the structural integrity of future Whitbread boats. Competition dictates that competitors will push boats to the limit and, with the large number of structural failures experienced in this Whitbread race, perhaps it is time to set stricter standards.

The casualty list included *Merit Cup*, which had her Satcom A dome stoved in when a large wave crashed on the foredeck. On board *Heineken*, Sue Crafer and Merritt Carey were abruptly woken as the water-ballast tank immediately alongside their bunks began to break free from the hull. The wayward water tank was not their only problem; the diesel tank was split open and precious fuel escaped into the bilge. The smell of diesel is nauseating enough at the best of times, but at sea in rough conditions it is enough to turn even the strongest stomach. If the fumes weren't enough to make the women ill, the fact that they were soon to break their rudder, in exactly the same place as it had failed on the previous leg, certainly would.

Initially, we lost only twenty miles to *Merit Cup* when we were forced off course to effect repairs to the hull, but as the wind and sea conditions moderated, we found ourselves well to the east of the bulk of the fleet. Over the next few days the weather favoured the boats in the west and the position reports showed us dropping further off the lead.

The cause of most of our frustrations was a series of black clouds, which reflected our mood. Each was like a huge vacuum, sucking up any wind for miles around. We took to calling these clouds black holes and it seemed there were more of them in this part of the Atlantic Ocean than in outer space. A vicious squall would herald the imminent arrival of a new cloud and within minutes we would be sitting becalmed again.

After three days of constant 'park-ups', we were 94 miles behind the leaders. The guys on *Intrum Justitia* couldn't believe how far back we had dropped and navigator Marcel Van Trieste faxed us to ask what was going on, saying they had placed odds amongst themselves as to whether we had dropped the mizzen mast again.

There was some humorous relief during the sched that evening as *Odessa* performed her obligation as duty yacht. After hearing several attempts to call up *Tokio* and *Dolphin and Youth*, Marcel tried to explain to the *Odessa* radio operator that the silent yachts were not currently racing and were in fact tied up in Brazilian ports. Marcel displayed his customary caustic wit suggesting that *Odessa*'s crew were demonstrating their 'Russian military efficiency'. Eugene Platon, the Ukrainian skipper of *Hetman Sahaidachny*, was quick to reply that it was 'more like KGB efficiency'.

BC won the British Telecom prize for the best video footage in the fleet.

We finally escaped the clutches of the black holes, broke out into the south-easterly trades and resumed our chase. With the conditions considerably steadier, we settled back into our regular watch system and concentrated on winding *New Zealand Endeavour* back up to full potential. The only excitement that occurred was when Nick slipped while walking around the interior of the boat in bare feet, slicing open the bottom of a foot in the process.

Nick's misfortune provided Trae with the opportunity he had been preparing for over the past five years. As Nick lay prone on the sails, Trae inspected the gash under the spotlight, with no shortage of amateur advice coming from the rest of the crew. There was an audible sigh of disappointment when Trae voiced his initial opinion that the cut may not require stitching. We don't know if Nick's foot really did need stitching, or whether Trae succumbed to the chorus of 'Stitch it! Stitch it!' from the gathering vultures. Whatever the reason, Trae finally got to put all of the years of training into practice as he proceeded to sew up the wound. Mindful of the fact that we were en route to America, the Mecca of medical litigation, Nick threatened Trae with legal action if the surgery wasn't up to scratch.

After a few days of relatively steady trade-wind sailing, we became reacquainted with the doldrums. According to all of the weather records and our own past experience, this phenomenon is considerably less intense on the western side of the Atlantic, along the Brazilian coast, than it is further east. While the doldrums had

'Dr Trae' prepares to stitch up Nick's cut foot with a gallery of concerned observers.

slowed down the fleet leaders and enabled us to close up somewhat, we still had to get through them ourselves. Picking our way through the maze of towering black cumulo-nimbus clouds, massive calms and persistent torrential rain was as much a case of luck as skill.

The whole fleet was to remain in the clutches of the doldrums for days, and fortunes were made and lost on a six-hourly basis as soon as the position scheds came in. It was very much a case of crossing your fingers and hoping you were in the right stretch of water. Normally relaxed people started to lose their patience and sense of humour as we sat becalmed in torrential rain for several hours on end. The constant 'slap, slap' of the sails being thrown from side to side by the swells and the slamming of waves under the stern were enough to try anyone's tolerance.

Midway across the doldrums we ghosted up to *Intrum Justitia*, who was having a particularly bad time. Marcel immediately called us on the VHF radio, warning us to 'Stay away — we attract no wind!' We should have paid heed. For hours we sat alongside *Intrum* while the opposition wriggled away from us. As we crossed back into the Northern Hemisphere, we reflected that we didn't even have anyone on board we could rake over in a line-crossing ceremony to vent our frustrations.

Drifting through the doldrums with yet another rain squall on the horizon.

Yamaha and *Merit Cup* were the first boats to escape into the trade winds, and for the next several days it was a case of the rich getting richer, the poor getting poorer. While we didn't appreciate it at the time, we were lucky to get out of the doldrums in the position we did. *Intrum Justitia*, *Galicia Pescanova* and *La Poste* were held captive for another day. If 'Huey' had not smiled on us, we could have easily lost the whole race right there in the doldrums.

Once into the trade winds, we experienced squally conditions for a couple of days. It was almost as if the doldrums were reaching out trying to pull us back in again. During a particularly dark early morning watch we were reaching along in twelve knots of air with the gennaker and mizzen staysail set, commenting on how pleasant it was to be back into steady conditions once more. In the space of ten seconds a 28-knot squall appeared from nowhere and thumped us with its full intensity. Before we knew what was going on, the boat was lying on its side, thrashing like a bronco.

There was no need to send anyone below to wake the off-watch; the thrashing of the sails had readily transmitted the message. We managed to get the big mizzen staysail rolled up and the boat back onto its feet again quickly. Once everything was back under control, Spike commented that he preferred the more conventional method of being woken up for the watch change.

The further we managed to get away from the doldrums, the steadier the breeze became as the trade winds asserted their dominance over all other weather patterns. After the frustrations we had recently experienced, no one was complaining about the monotony. With the wind rarely shifting more than a few degrees or changing in strength by more than a couple of knots, there were few sail changes — a rare pleasure on board a ketch.

After the cold night watches in the Southern Ocean, it was bliss to be able to come on deck in the middle of the night dressed in nothing more than a pair of shorts and a T-shirt. The days of taking twenty minutes to get dressed to come on watch were starting to seem like a very distant memory. The telling factor, confirming how pleasant the conditions were, was when BC started coming on deck for extended periods in the middle of the night without being asked.

More than a thousand miles astern of us, *Tokio* and *Dolphin and Youth* had rejoined the race once more after their unscheduled stops in Brazil. We found it hard to imagine how they could find the motivation to continue on to Fort Lauderdale now that they were effectively out of the race for the major placings. Upon their arrival in Florida, the *Tokio* crew were naturally very dispirited and we learnt that they had taken things easy for the remainder of leg five.

Ironically for the crew of *Dolphin and Youth*, they found that their delamination problem was not as extreme as they had first thought. A structural engineer and boat builder had flown out from Europe to meet them at Rio de Janeiro and assess the damage to the hull. They discovered that the core was still intact and the extent of the delamination was not serious. With no deep-water berthing available, Humphries

and his crew had to moor their boat 100 metres off the dock, with a power lead for the compressor and heater running across to the shore. While they hurriedly repaired their wounded boat, the race was still at full pace in the Northern Hemisphere.

The steady fresh trade winds were proving to be very much to *Yamaha's* liking, and Ross Field, in conjunction with Nik White, was doing a good job of keeping his boat in the right part of the ocean. As the race was progressing, the Whitbread 60s were being steadily optimised for the lighter winds. Their light-weight drifter sail, which was originally intended to be used in only the very lightest of winds, was being flown in up to twelve knots of breeze, generating immense power and producing spectacular performance gains.

Once into the trade winds, the tactical options available to the navigators became minimal. The steady winds effectively closed down any passing lanes and the fastest route to the finish was a straight line. It was shaping up to be a drag race, but the problem was that it had effectively begun on the northern side of the doldrums, with the leaders at that stage having a massive advantage.

As we reached across the northern coast of Brazil, past the mouth of the Amazon River, all we could do was hope that *Yamaha* and *Merit Cup* would get held up by a high-pressure system nearer Florida. Things were starting to look a little grim for us, as *Yamaha* extended her lead over *Endeavour* to a whopping 190 miles and we were in danger of losing our overall lead to the flying blue-hulled Whitbread 60. Fehlman

Back into the trade winds again, New Zealand Endeavour *powers up in pursuit of* Yamaha *and* Merit Cup.

and company had been dropped by *Yamaha*, but were still 60 miles ahead of us.

In the previous Whitbread race, *Steinlager 2* and *Fisher and Paykel* had enjoyed a significant edge over their rivals in conditions that permitted fully powered-up reaching. Even though *Endeavour* was significantly quicker than her predecessors, she was unable to foot it with the water-ballasted 60s in those same conditions. It almost felt at times as if we were carrying a blunt knife in a gun fight.

To break up the routine of our watches, we engaged in a trivia contest over the Satcom C with the women on *Heineken*. The level of general knowledge was impressive and after a few days the questions became increasingly difficult. Having been caught out on a couple of obscure questions, such as who is the manager of the Finnish ice-hockey team, we decided to play hard ball and asked them to name the entire All Black team for the 1987 Rugby World Cup. We were supremely confident of having outsmarted them. But the next day they faxed their reply to us and, much to our horror, answered correctly. Even though they had a Kiwi, Leah Newbold, on board, we were convinced that they had acquired some outside assistance.

In keeping with our policy of sailing this leg as light as we possibly could, BC had brought along a minimal amount of sunblock. As we sat burning to a crisp in the intense sunlight, BC bore the brunt of some pointed comments from the rest of the crew. Our stocks were so limited that we only had enough to apply to our faces. While some of the fairer-skinned guys, like Moose and Trev, were suffering under this strict rationing, Burt was not at all concerned. With Fort Lauderdale and its many attractions looming ever closer, he was working on the perfect all-over tan, going as

Ross Field and his Yamaha *team sailed a flawless leg to Florida to take the overall lead in the 60s class.*

far as wearing his watch on the opposite wrist to ensure he didn't have a tan line. When questioned about this, Burt mumbled something unlikely about a heat rash developing beneath his watch strap.

Nick was evidently suffering some sort of an identity crisis and wasn't sure whether he fitted into the *Bay Watch* mould or whether he was more inclined towards a Bavarian image. This came about when he decided to cut the legs off his wet-weather trousers in an effort to stay cool in the searing tropical heat. In the face of howls of derision from the rest of the crew, Nick steadfastly insisted that he was a trend-setter. Despite Nick's assurances, the rest of us just couldn't believe that his alternative lederhosen would ever become *de rigueur* on the decks of racing yachts.

Although *Yamaha* was still a long way out in front of us, life wasn't too bad as we rounded the island of Barbuda on the outer extremities of the Caribbean. With a course change of 30 degrees, we were able to set our spinnaker and mizzen gennaker for the run down outside the magnificent Virgin Islands. It seemed criminal that we were racing past them without having a closer look. That is probably the major frustration of the Whitbread race — you're forever sailing past interesting places without stopping.

Being pulled along by the cloud of downwind sail, *New Zealand Endeavour* was lifting her heels in pursuit of the leading duo. For the first time in over a week, the boats behind were gaining an advantage over those further to the north-west. As we had hoped, the high-pressure system that is often to be found over the southern tip of Florida and the Bahamas was present and *Yamaha*'s progress was being impeded by light winds.

Suddenly the world didn't seem such a bad place after all. We were enjoying some superb sailing through the tropics and the pendulum seemed to be swinging in our favour for the first time since leaving Punta almost three weeks ago. *Yamaha* was clearly going to win the leg into Fort Lauderdale, of that there was little doubt. Our mission was to reduce the deficit by every minute we could to ensure we started the last leg with a comfortable buffer over them. With 500 miles between us and the finish line, *Yamaha* was down to a 94-mile lead and *Merit Cup* was 34 miles ahead of us.

We were counting our blessings that we had not encountered any further strong head winds to stress the damaged section of hull. The predominantly downwind and reaching conditions meant the boat did not bang or slam off waves, but while we were reflecting on that piece of good fortune, it became apparent that the rudder was becoming increasingly difficult to turn. Initially we thought there must be some sort of flotsam jammed between the rudder and the hull. Closer inspection revealed that the problem lay within the bottom rudder bearing, imbedded in the hull.

The possible implications of this discovery were extremely serious. If we had to go close reaching in fresh winds where the rudder would load up, there was a very real possibility that the rudder would seize up, making the boat impossible to steer.

Next page: A 27,000-kilo maxi tosses a lot of water out of its way.

There was no way of replacing or repairing the damaged bearings, and all we could do was hope that we didn't encounter too much wind before the finish.

Lady Luck was to continue smiling on us for the remainder of the leg. Light winds not only kept our potential steering problem at bay, they allowed us to continue winding in the leaders. By the time we entered the Providence Channel for the final leg of the journey in through the Bahamas, we had closed to within 75 miles of *Yamaha* and twenty behind *Merit Cup*. *Intrum Justitia* had slipped back a comfortable 50 miles astern of us.

We spent the final day gybing our way down the Providence Channel in tropical thunderstorms dodging cruise ships. Visibility was often cut down to less than a mile as the rolling black clouds enveloped us and torrential rain drowned the boat. We could scarcely believe our eyes, or good fortune, when the clouds dissipated to reveal *Merit Cup* on the horizon ahead of us. After sixteen days of playing catch-up, it was satisfying to have them in sight again. Less enthused were the Swiss crew, who had been hoping to make a telling break on us in our injured state. As on leg two, they had been unable to take advantage of our predicament and make any real impact on our overall lead.

Crossing the Gulf Stream, which separates the Bahamas from Florida, is always

A trip onto the foredeck in the tropics is a considerably more pleasant experience than it is in the Southern Ocean.

a tricky exercise as the fast-flowing current can considerably slow a boat's progress. Ross Field and his team on *Yamaha* had arrived in Fort Lauderdale earlier that afternoon. They had sailed an impressive leg and, given *Tokio*'s demise, were now well in control of the Whitbread 60 class for the Heineken Trophy. As night fell, *Merit Cup* disappeared from view into the darkness and it became obvious that there was no way we were going to catch them before the finish.

New Zealand Endeavour eventually slipped across the finish line at the entrance to Port Everglade shortly after midnight, 45 minutes behind *Merit Cup*. *Yamaha* had beaten us to Florida by a margin of eight hours. Considering the deficit we had been facing a week earlier, we were happy with our result.

With the final sprint to England ahead, we now had a lead of eighteen hours on *Merit Cup* and almost twelve on *Yamaha* for overall elapsed time. However, one lesson we had learnt on this supposedly easy leg was that the race was far from over.

Leg Five: Punta Del Este — Fort Lauderdale (5475 miles)

Class	Boat Name	Days	Hours	Minutes	Secs	Overall Position After Leg	Average Speed for Leg
W 60	*Yamaha*	22	05	13	50	2	10.1
Maxi	*Merit Cup*	22	12	30	00	3	10.0
Maxi	*New Zealand Endeavour*	22	13	15	53	1	10.0
W 60	*Intrum Justitia*	22	19	16	48	4	9.8
W 60	*Galicia 93 Pescanova*	23	03	49	04	5	9.7
W 60	*Winston*	23	05	10	53	6	9.7
W 60	*Brooksfield*	23	09	31	58	9	9.6
Maxi	*La Poste*	23	16	08	11	7	9.5
W 60	*Heineken*	24	05	23	15	10	9.3
W 60	*Hetman Sahaidachny*	24	19	10	36	11	9.1
Maxi	*Uruguay Natural*	26	07	22	49	13	8.5
W 60	*Odessa*	26	15	42	31	14	8.4
W 60	*Dolphin and Youth*	28	03	10	57	12	8.0
W 60	*Tokio*	31	01	48	21	8	7.2

CHAPTER TEN

The Home Straight

'Welcome to the United States of America!' the Customs man yelled as he clambered on board *New Zealand Endeavour* while we motored up the harbour to the Heineken Village. Whenever we arrived in port at the completion of a leg, the first priority was to clear Customs and Immigration in much the same way that is required when arriving at an international airport. By the time we had arrived at the dock, Mike had convinced the Customs official that we were not 'illegal aliens' or undercover cocaine traffickers.

For some of the crew, it was to be a reunion with families and wives they hadn't seen since leaving Auckland several months previously. After the difficulties of language and culture in Uruguay, Florida felt more like home. Being able to walk into a restaurant and order a meal off an English menu was considerably more comfortable than some of our experiences in Punta. Throughout our month-long stopover in Fort Lauderdale we all stayed in the same motel complex, complete with swimming pool.

Annie Hodgkinson's daily routine of shopping for 30 hungry people was a breeze after Uruguay, where the only choice had been T-bone steaks or spicy sausages. After a month of freeze-dried sustenance, the crew saw to it that the local pizza shop and McDonald's did a roaring trade.

The local race organisers had done an admirable job of setting up a brand-new regatta village and mooring facilities. These were every bit the equal of Auckland's Viaduct Basin, though they didn't achieve anything like the same carnival atmosphere. Although there had been considerable promotion and advertising, there was not the same level of public interest that the race enjoys in New Zealand and Europe. The American sporting public have some vague idea what the America's Cup is all about, but when it comes to the Whitbread, the usual response is, 'Huh!, what's the White-bread race?'

Within a day of arriving in Fort Lauderdale we moved *New Zealand Endeavour* up to Derecktor Gunnell's, the local boat yard catering to the mega-yachts and power boats that proliferate in Florida. The work list Shoebie had written up on our arrival in port was extensive, with the delamination problem at the top. Because of the magnitude and importance of this repair, George was assisted by an American boat builder to ensure that it all got done in time. Within days of the fleet finishing the leg, Derecktor Gunnell's began to take on the appearance of a hospital casualty ward for sick boats. Almost every boat had suffered varying degrees of delamination during the gale off Brazil. Russell Bowler from the Farr design office was on hand to provide the prescriptions.

In addition to the repairs necessary to get *Endeavour* back into perfect condition, a thorough preventative maintenance programme was put in place. The sixth leg had been brutal on the boats in the previous race. With this in mind, we went over every

Brad adjusts the tack of the mizzen gennaker.

bolt, fitting and connection with a fine-tooth comb, looking for the slightest fault. During this process, a significant dent was discovered near the top of the main mast, which could have resulted in a broken spar.

While the boat was in the shed, George took the opportunity to pull the lead bulb off the bottom of the keel to check its integrity. Although we only had just over ten per cent of the race remaining we took no shortcuts in the all-important preparation. We sanded the bottom of the boat and repainted it to ensure the hull finish was as fast as possible.

While the boat yard resounded to the sounds of power tools and sandpaper, the alarm bells were ringing at full volume over at the race headquarters. Within days of stepping ashore after winning the fifth leg, Ross Field and his Ocean Ventures partners were faced with a multi-million-dollar writ from Nance Frank claiming defamation and misappropriation of funds. The drama had begun when Frank, skipper of the ill-fated *US Women's Challenge*, withdrew from the race at the conclusion of the first leg. Ocean Ventures, the company that managed the *Yamaha* campaign, then repossessed Frank's boat (the former *Yamaha 1*) and hired Dawn Riley to continue racing the boat, renamed *Heineken*, with the same core crew.

Frank was not only suing Ocean Ventures, she also served writs on Heineken and the Whitbread race organisers, citing collusion to force her out of the race. To many observers this seemed to be nothing more than a case of sour grapes. When *Heineken* finished in Fort Lauderdale to a big welcome, one of Frank's original investors was arrested for abusive behaviour in public.

Frank really stirred up a hornets' nest when she produced a series of transcripts, allegedly from her yacht's Satcom C to *Yamaha*, that suggested the passing of weather information between Field and his girlfriend, Adrienne Cahalan, who was navigator on the all-women's boat. The racing rules clearly state that no yacht may receive any outside assistance, so if Frank's allegations were proved, the consequences would be extremely serious.

Frank had given some of these transcripts to Ian Bailey-Wilmott, the Whitbread race director, at the time she withdrew from the race. He felt that it would be impossible to verify their authenticity and had taken no further action. But now the heat was being turned up and Bailey-Wilmott was compelled to request a convening of the International Jury to investigate the matter.

After the less-than-convincing performance by the jury during the *Brooksfield* redress hearings, there was considerable interest in their handling of this case. The jury, however, seemed to dismiss it perfunctorily, apparently on the grounds that British Telecom, who handled the Satcom transmissions, could not verify the authenticity of the transcripts. Nevertheless, it was astounding that none of the major players was called to give any evidence, and for Field and Cahalan, it must have been frustrating not to have the opportunity to clear their names.

Some of the skippers, notably Dennis Conner, were unimpressed with the jury's decision not to hear the case. With the increasing level of money being invested in

the Whitbread race, and the increasing focus of the media, it is essential for the sake of the sport that the race organisers and the International Jury get their act together in the future.

Meanwhile, on the other side of town, *New Zealand Endeavour* was being put back together again after her thorough medical. With the bulk of the job list completed, the sailing crew took a week's break to have a look around Florida. The popular destinations were the Florida Keys, Cape Canaveral and the impressive Walt Disney World in Orlando. Shoebie and his wife Sally took their two-year-old son to meet the Disney characters, but after all the hype and battling the crowds for hours they were exasperated when Thomas asked, 'When can we go to Disneyland?'

One activity that has gained huge popularity in Florida is roller blading. Dalts was not at all impressed with this pastime, considering it to be 'marginal' behaviour. When a rumour started circulating around the boat yard that he had been seen out roller blading along the beach front, Dalts became distraught trying to convince everyone that it wasn't him. Even though we knew that he hadn't joined the trendsetters in their skin-tight lycra shorts, we were all having far too much fun winding him up to let it go.

During the Fort Lauderdale stopover, all of the race crews got together for this photo.

While the boat had been out of the water, Mike had immersed himself in the task of getting to understand the complexities of the Gulf Stream, which were sure to be major factors in the first half of the leg across the Atlantic. This current originates in the Atlantic and is caused by the persistent trade winds generating a northwards flow of water in the Caribbean, up through the Straits of Florida and back into the north Atlantic. The Gulf Stream is a body of very warm water that behaves like a meandering river, with the strongest current in the middle and opposing eddies on the edges.

Its position changes on a daily basis, so it is critical to keep up-to-date with its movements. It is common for yachts to come up against a strong adverse flow when the navigator thinks they should be riding a favourable current.

In the days leading up to the restart, it was becoming evident that we were going to be faced with head winds in the early stages of the sixth leg. This is usually of no great concern, but it was disconcerting that on this occasion we would be sailing up the Gulf Stream in a big seaway and these were the conditions in which the last Whitbread fleet had staged an impromptu demolition derby.

After a month of enjoying the good life in America, we swung back into focus on start day. Dalts had been immersed in negotiations for the sale of *New Zealand Endeavour*, the contract for which was signed within minutes of our departure. Perhaps it was due to this last-minute distraction that we made our worst start of the race. It took us too long to get our act together in the variable conditions and we rounded

New Zealand Endeavour *lines up with* Tokio *on the start line off Fort Lauderdale.*

the first mark in poor shape. However, within an hour a large wind shift and the influence of the Gulf Stream had everyone back on an even footing.

With up to three knots of current running against a 25-knot head wind on our first night back at sea, we got a rude awakening after a spell of basking in the sun and enjoying eight-hour sleeps. Not for the first time, it dawned on us that the shore crew were actually the smart ones. While we were out at sea crashing off steep waves, they were back at the motel enjoying a few beers beside the swimming pool. Many of us swore if we were going to do the Whitbread again, it would be as a member of the shore crew flying between ports to meet the boat.

We did not have too long to reflect on that luxury, as a major split was occurring in the fleet. Two distinct options seemed available. We could abandon our pre-race strategy of staying in the Gulf Stream and instead make a run for it straight down the rhumb-line towards England, or we could accept that we would suffer big losses initially by sailing the extra distance to stay in the Stream. There were strong arguments for each option, but after a lengthy debate Dalts decided to stick with the Gulf Stream.

All the leading Whitbread 60s were of the same inclination and tacked onto starboard to dig back into the Stream, while *Merit Cup*, *Brooksfield* and *Galicia Pescanova* took the bull by the horns and continued sailing down the rhumb line. With over eighteen hours to catch up, Pierre Fehlman had no option but to try and play a wild card. We knew that our position scheds would not look good for a while, but our hearts were in our mouths as *Merit Cup* extended the lead to 100 miles.

The weather maps were indicating more favourable wind in the north-west, with less further to the east, where Fehlman was. After the fresh conditions of the first night, the breeze had lightened considerably and we ghosted along in light air for the next two days while *Merit Cup* stretched her legs. Much to our relief, the decision to stay in the Gulf Stream started to pay dividends on the fifth day at sea. The promised westerlies began to build and, combined with the shunt the Stream was giving us, we rocketed out into the North Atlantic.

The big question was whether the loss we had incurred would be too much to overcome. Even though we were now making fast progress, the decision to stay in the Stream had been compounding on a daily basis and *Merit Cup* was now enjoying a massive advantage of 152 miles. If the wind swung through to the east in the latter stages of the leg, giving us head winds, Fehlman's margin could be enough to win the race outright.

With this prospect playing heavily on our minds, we kept our huge mizzen gennaker up in the steadily increasing wind. With the assistance of nearly six knots of current, *New Zealand Endeavour* was flying towards England and for long periods of time our speed across the bottom never dropped below twenty knots.

Whenever Mike poked his head out through the aft hatch he was asked, 'How long will these running conditions last?' He became very popular when he announced

Next page: A large Gulf Stream wave obscures New Zealand Endeavour *as we power upwind away from the Florida coast.*

that the weather maps were indicating that we would have these tail winds for most of the trip across the Atlantic.

Even though we had a lot of catching up to do on the leading trio, *Endeavour* was 56 miles ahead of the nearest boat behind us. Although we were starting to get quite well north, the air was still warm and water temperatures in the Gulf Stream were up to 28 degrees.

A natural hazard associated with warm water is the abundance of flying fish, and although we were well north of the tropics, there were still a few to be found. A particularly large specimen was out for an afternoon's recreation when its flight path coincided with our deck. The fish performed a series of spectacular aerobatics in an attempt to avoid a collision, but misjudged its trajectory and scored a direct hit between BC's eyes. Debate raged over who was more stunned — BC or the flying fish.

Earlier that morning the visibility had been down to 400 metres, with a thick haze surrounding us. Bursting through this at over 25 knots, we discovered company in the form of a US Navy destroyer. We spoke to them on the VHF radio and learnt that they were heading across the Atlantic to take part in the D-Day celebrations.

The concern shows on Mike and Foxy's faces as the sched shows Merit Cup *out to a lead of 151 miles.*

After slowing down for a brief look at us, we heard their powerful gas turbines wind up and they rapidly disappeared off into the haze.

By day six we were 300 miles off the coast of Nova Scotia on our great circle course to England. We were still enjoying the benefit of the Gulf Stream and at last the scheds seemed to be showing that our course was becoming the Yellow Brick Road. In one six-hour period, we had pulled 31 miles out of *Merit Cup* to bring her lead down to 104 miles. *Yamaha* was back to 98 miles astern, but with 2400 miles between us and Southampton there was a lot of racing to do yet. With the assistance of the Stream, *New Zealand Endeavour* was really stretching her legs and we had just recorded a 24-hour run of 403 miles.

If we were experiencing a dream ride, the leading trio certainly were not. Having made what initially looked like being a leg-winning break, *Merit Cup*, *Brooksfield* and *Galicia Pescanova* were starting to come unstuck to the south of us. Their nemesis was a large cell of high pressure, which had left them flopping around in light winds while the rest of the fleet were riding fresh westerlies in a 'river' of wind between two weather systems.

Fehlman had the opportunity to consolidate his lead by cutting back to the north, but had not done so and would come to rue his decision. Over the next two days, *Merit Cup* was to lose her 100-mile advantage as she continued to languish in the light winds.

Our magic-carpet ride through the Gulf Stream was about to come to an end. While our great circle course to England would require climbing up to a latitude of at least 50 degrees North, the Stream takes an abrupt turn back to the south-east again when it meets the icy Labrador Current.

It was a rude awakening to be plunged back into near-freezing conditions once more. Over the period of one watch, we went from wearing shorts and T-shirts to full thermal and wet-weather gear. Accompanying this abrupt change in temperature was a dense layer of fog, which reduced visibility to little more than a boat length and demanded a constant watch on the radar.

The Labrador Current brings down a proliferation of icebergs from the Arctic Circle, so it was disconcerting to be charging through a pea-souper under full spinnaker and mizzen gennaker, knowing that large chunks of ice were floating in the neighbourhood. If one of these bergs had been able to sink the *Titanic* in this same stretch of water, we would have no hope of surviving a prang. Although we detected only one iceberg on the radar, further to the north of us *Intrum Justitia* reported dodging them constantly. Adding to our concern was the fact that the Newfoundland Banks we were sailing across are heavily populated fishing grounds. The prospect of charging into a trawler's net also held limited appeal.

Once we had overtaken *Merit Cup*, 120 miles to the south, *New Zealand Endeavour* had her nose in front for the first time in the leg. The bulk of the fleet was following the same track as us, with the exception of *Intrum Justitia*. Lawrie Smith and his experienced navigator Marcel Van Trieste decided to take a gamble by sailing

well to the north in search of stronger winds. For a couple of days their punt seemed to be paying dividends, until the low-pressure system ran out of puff.

Although we worked hard to maintain our 45-mile advantage, we began to be held up by a weak front that was creeping along ahead of us. Each time we caught up with this, the spinnaker would collapse back into the rig and we would stall. No sooner were we picked up by the breeze again than we would crash back into the frustrating calm. In the space of a day, *Yamaha* and *Tokio* came charging over the horizon and suddenly three boats were within a mile of each other, with *Winston* not far behind. Fortunately, a moderate westerly tail wind picked up and we were able to sail away to a four-mile lead during the night.

Dawn on our penultimate day at sea brought a steady increase in wind strength, which soon had *Tokio* and *Yamaha* powering up to draw level with us. As the wind came slowly forward until we were close reaching, we went through the all-too-familiar frenzy of sail changing. Several of the crew on *Tokio* and *Yamaha* later commented that they were astounded at how many changes we had to go through to keep the ketch 'in the groove'. While the 60s only had to drop their reaching gennakers and hoist a jib-top reaching headsail, *Endeavour*'s insatiable appetite for complicated sail combinations resulted in no fewer than seven sail changes.

As we approached the south coast of Ireland in the early afternoon, Mike pre-

It requires sheer grunt to haul the foot of the mainsail across after reefing.

dicted the arrival of a strong frontal system accompanied by 45-knot winds and rain. The rest of the crew thought he was laying it on a bit thick when he announced that this would hit at 1500 hours. With the 60s alongside us, the last thing we wanted were strong reaching conditions. However, the sky astern of us began to grow ominously dark and, right on cue, the front slammed into us. As Mike stuck his head out of the aft hatch to gloat over his accurate prediction he found an inattentive audience. Everyone was too busy changing and reefing sails trying to keep the boat on its feet.

The bowmen have the toughest job in these conditions. As *Endeavour* sliced through the foaming grey water of the Irish Sea, Sean and Burt were perched up on the narrow bow, wrestling the wildly flapping headsail back down the headfoil. This in itself is physically very demanding, without the added threat of walls of water surging over the clipper bow with the force of an express train. In addition to keeping themselves on board, they had to ensure the breaking seas didn't wash the headsail overboard. Assisting the bowmen were crew from the standby watch who formed a line along the foredeck and helped pull the sail down. Tethered to the deck with safety harnesses, they were often picked up by a wave and washed back against the mast.

As dusk enveloped us, we watched with awe as *Tokio* and *Yamaha* turned on

Sean enjoying life on the bow during a headsail change.

an impressive display of what this new generation of ocean greyhounds is capable of. With full water ballast and shortened sail, they sat up and scorched away from us, averaging a full two knots more boat speed. As we trimmed *Endeavour*'s sails in response to the wind and waves, we reflected that while the IOR maxi ketches are impressive and graceful boats, their days as the premier Whitbread ocean racers were very nearly over.

During the second stopover in Punta del Este, the Whitbread committee had announced that the next race would feature only 60s. Although many would agree that the design concept of the 60s is clearly the way of the future, it was a shame to think that the perennial maxis were about to become extinct. There is no doubt that the awesome spectacle of a huge maxi fully powered up beneath clouds of sail has captured the public's imagination and helped to make the Whitbread race what it is today.

After a torrid night of heavy seas whipped up by winds gusting to 50 knots, we were more than happy to see the bleak cliff faces of Land's End appearing through a cool and hazy English dawn. Throughout the night the leading 60s, which now included *Winston*, had stretched out to a 20-mile lead over us and, with a blistering

Any misconceptions we may have been harbouring about an easy finish were shattered when a 50-knot front hammered us on our last night at sea.

run down the English Channel coming up, there was no chance of our catching them before the finish. Although we were not going to win the final leg, our overall lead was still well in hand and the last thing we needed was a dropped rig or any other terminal mishap.

As soon as we rounded the surf-engulfed Land's End, Shoebie called for his watch to set up the spinnaker. While Spike set the chute up on the bow, Trae tailed the halyard up and cleated it off. With a resounding crack the spinnaker burst open, heralding the start of what was to be one of our fastest downwind rides in the whole race. As each line squall came hurtling down the Channel and picked us up, the boat speed surged, as did the concentration of the helmsman and trimmer. In some

The early dawn light illuminates the deck as we scorch up the English Channel towards the finish.

ways, it seemed appropriate that we should finish the Whitbread in these conditions. Fast and tough sailing is the essence of what makes the 33,000-mile race so special.

While *New Zealand Endeavour* was smoking down the Channel, Chris Dickson and his team on *Tokio* were turning on a stunning show of boat speed. While the dismasting on the previous leg had probably robbed them of overall victory in the Whitbread 60 class, they could at least complete their race on a high note. The predominantly Kiwi crew on *Winston* were evidently in the same frame of mind as they blasted into the Solent in second place to give them fourth overall in the Whitbread 60 class.

Ironically, after circling the globe, we achieved our fastest speed of the entire race as we approached the entrance to the Solent, when Foxy aimed *Endeavour* down a couple of steep waves, letting gravity do all of the work as the speed dial climbed to 28.8 knots.

With less than 25 miles to the finish, we approached the hazardous Needles on the western end of the Isle of Wight. The passage through the Needles into the Solent is, in places, no more than 100 metres wide. On a maxi travelling down breaking seas at close to twenty knots, squeezing through that is enough to give even the most relaxed person a serious case of heart palpitations. Dalts ordered the spinnaker dropped in readiness for a gybe as we approached the narrow gap, but with shallow water and breaking surf fast approaching, the sail would not release. Panic-stricken calls of 'Get rid of it!' were met with an equally shrill response: 'I can't, the clips jammed closed!' With less than 50 metres to spare, the spinnaker was tripped away and Dalts crash gybed the boat through the passage.

Once into the relative safety of the Solent, the spinnaker was reset for a rapid transit down to Cowes. With gusts of 45 knots, we were enjoying our last few miles on *New Zealand Endeavour*. Not only had she taken us through the toughest oceans in the world, she had been our home for 120 days as we battled against the opposition and the elements.

It was a nice touch that, as we dropped the spinnaker and altered course for the last eight miles up Southampton Water to the finish, we should be escorted by the magnificent *QE 2*. Under a heavily reefed rig, *New Zealand Endeavour* heeled in response to the gusts as the bow sliced through the water for a last charge to the finish line. On deck we continued trimming to keep the boat at full pace as the end of our circumnavigation rapidly approached. At 1510 GMT, a loud cannon blast signalled that *New Zealand Endeavour* had won the maxi class of the 1993/94 Whitbread race.

As we began to lower the sails for the last time, we had time to pause for a moment's reflection. Not only had we won the Heineken Trophy for the maxi class, we had set the fastest elapsed time of the Whitbread race, smashing *Steinlager 2*'s record by more than eight days. Ross Field's *Yamaha* had finished two hours earlier to win the Heineken Trophy for the Whitbread 60 class and confirm New Zealand's

Previous pages: The magnificent QE 2 *accompanies* New Zealand Endeavour *up Southampton water to the finish line.*

domination of this round-the-world marathon. It did not go unnoticed by the world's press that the first four yachts to finish the final leg into Southampton were all skippered by New Zealanders.

Considering the inclement weather we arrived in, we were amazed by the number of Kiwis lining the dock at Ocean Village to cheer us into the pontoon. If ever we had forgotten about the level of support we had from our compatriots, the reception they gave us as we were presented with the Heineken Trophy soon reminded us of our debt. Most of those who had been instrumental in *New Zealand Endeavour*'s success were on hand to help us celebrate with an enormous party on board for all of our fellow New Zealand competitors. It seemed fitting that our magnificent white ketch should play host to this group of world-beating Kiwis.

For all of us, the finish produced mixed emotions. On the one hand, we couldn't wait to get off the boat; on the other, it was hard to contemplate the break-up of what had become an extended family. There is nothing more over than when the Whitbread ends. Having lived, eaten and thought of little else for the past two years, it comes as a bit of a shock when it all suddenly stops.

Competing in the Whitbread means different things to different people. For Dalts,

It had taken 33,000 miles and nine months, but finally the Heineken Trophy and new Whitbread record for the fastest circumnavigation were ours!

it was the culmination of a desire to have his own winning campaign that had been burning since his introduction to the Whitbread in 1981. For many of the younger guys, it was the chance of a lifetime to be part of a high-profile project. Sean perhaps best summed up the feeling: 'It's a race of extreme highs and lows, awesome experiences and memories, but also long periods of hard, wet, boring sailing.'

The race changes those who compete in it. For some of the guys, it's hard to settle back into a conventional lifestyle. The challenge and excitement of racing at breakneck speed through the most demanding oceans in the world is, for some people, addictive. Undoubtedly, many will take up the challenge again in the future.

The 1993–94 Whitbread had proved to be all the *Endeavour* team had hoped for. From the highs of pushing the boat right to the edge — and occasionally beyond it — to the depressing days of breaking our mizzen mast in the depths of the Southern Ocean, we had endured and finished the race as great friends.

Whatever may lie ahead, the camaraderie and achievements of the team will never be forgotten by those of us who were part of *New Zealand Endeavour*.

Leg Six: Fort Lauderdale — Southampton (3818 miles)

Class	Boat Name	Days	Hours	Minutes	Secs	Finishing Position for Leg	Average Speed for Leg
W 60	*Tokio*	12	19	36	27	1	12.4
W 60	*Winston*	12	20	27	00	2	12.4
W 60	*Yamaha*	12	20	57	25	3	12.4
Maxi	*New Zealand Endeavour*	12	22	55	07	4	12.3
W 60	*Intrum Justitia*	13	01	02	49	5	12.2
Maxi	*Merit Cup*	13	02	15	35	6	12.2
Maxi	*La Poste*	13	06	35	59	7	12.0
W 60	*Reebok*	13	07	34	21	8	12.0
W 60	*Galicia 93 Pescanova*	13	09	28	18	9	11.9
W 60	*Brooksfield*	14	01	00	36	10	11.4
W 60	*Hetman Sahaidachny*	14	16	49	47	11	10.6
W 60	*Odessa*	15	17	40	11	12	10.1
Maxi	*Uruguay Natural*	16	13	27	41	13	9.6
W 60	*Heineken*	18	06	14	07	14	9.2

What all the fuss had been about - the Heineken Trophy.

1993/94 WHITBREAD ROUND THE WORLD RACE RESULTS
(32,926 miles)

Class	Boat Name	Days	Hours	Minutes	Secs	Overall Finishing Position	Average Speed for Race
Maxi	*New Zealand Endeavour*	120	05	09	23	1	11.21
W 60	*Yamaha*	120	14	55	00	2	11.17
Maxi	*Merit Cup*	121	02	50	47	3	11.12
W 60	*Intrum Justitia*	121	05	26	26	4	11.11
W 60	*Galicia 93 Pescanova*	122	06	12	23	5	11.02
W 60	*Winston*	122	09	32	09	6	11.0
Maxi	*La Poste*	123	22	54	58	7	10.87
W 60	*Tokio*	128	16	19	48	8	10.47
W 60	*Brooksfield*	130	04	29	27	9	10.35
W 60	*Hetman Sahaidachny*	135	23	17	52	10	9.9
W 60	*Heineken*	136	22	30	51	11	9.84
W 60	*Reebok*	137	21	03	17	12	9.77
Maxi	*Uruguay Natural*	145	00	17	44	13	9.29
W 60	*Odessa*	158	04	34	40	14	8.51

NEW ZEALAND ENDEAVOUR SPONSORS

SPONSORS
ANZ Banking Group (NZ) Ltd
BP Oil New Zealand Ltd
Health Sponsorship Council, in conjunction with
   the Sports Foundation Inc.
Clear Communications Ltd
Toyota New Zealand Ltd
The Apple and Pear Marketing Board — ENZA
The New Zealand Lotteries Commission Instant Kiwi
Television New Zealand — Official Broadcaster

LEVEL TWO SUPPLIERS
Panasonic
Altex Coatings
Volpower New Zealand Ltd
Pan Print
Morgan and Banks
Multi Media Systems
Trimble Navigation
RFD New Zealand Ltd
Griffiths McKay Ltd
Kodak New Zealand Ltd

LEVEL ONE SUPPLIERS
KPMG Peat Marwick
Russell McVeagh McKenzie Bartleet

Canterbury International Ltd
P & O Containers

THE 1993–94 WHITBREAD RO

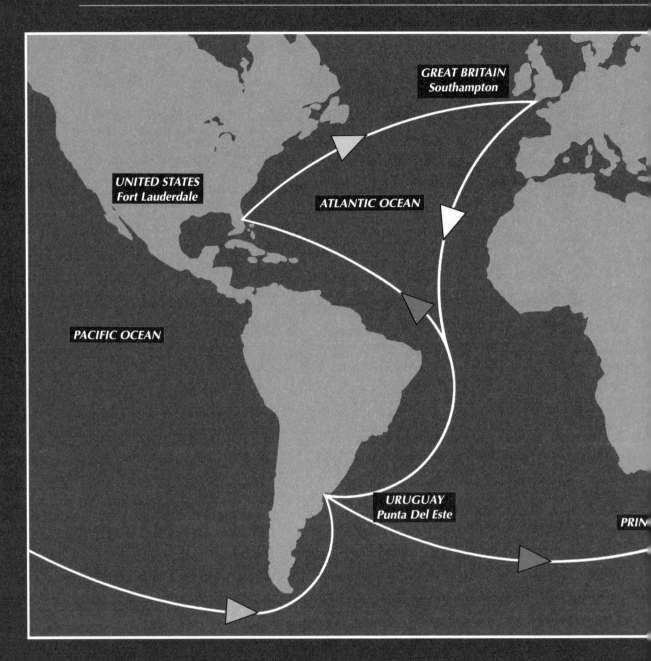

GREAT BRITAIN
Southampton

UNITED STATES
Fort Lauderdale

ATLANTIC OCEAN

PACIFIC OCEAN

URUGUAY
Punta Del Este

PRIN

▶ Leg 1
5938 Nautical Miles
SOUTHAMPTON to
PUNTA DEL ESTE (URUGUAY)

▶ Leg 2
7558 Nautical Miles
PUNTA DEL ESTE to
FREMANTLE (AUSTRALIA)

▶ Leg 3
3272 Nautical Miles
FREMANTLE to
AUCKLAND (NEW ZEALAND)